APPETITE

APPETITE

A MEMOIR IN RECIPES OF
FAMILY AND FOOD

ED BALLS

GALLERY BOOKS UK

First published in Great Britain by Gallery Books,
an imprint of Simon & Schuster UK Ltd, 2021

3 5 7 9 10 8 6 4 2

Simon & Schuster UK Ltd
1st Floor
222 Gray's Inn Road
London WC1X 8HB

www.simonandschuster.co.uk
www.simonandschuster.com.au
www.simonandschuster.co.in

Simon & Schuster Australia, Sydney
Simon & Schuster India, New Delhi

A CIP catalogue record for this book
is available from the British Library

Hardback ISBN: 978-1-3985-0474-5
eBook ISBN: 978-1-3985-0475-2

Typeset in Bembo by M Rules
Printed and bound by CPI Group (UK) Ltd, Croydon, CR0 4YY

For my mum, who taught me to love cooking . . .

. . . and my dad, who taught me to love eating

Contents

Introduction

My Life and Roast Beef

All the family round the table, laughing and bickering. Roast beef, pink but not rare. Plenty of gravy, rich and spicy with a hint of red wine. Heaps of Yorkshire puddings, clean out of the tin. Steam rising from the carrots, broccoli and cabbage. And shiny roast potatoes, crispy on the outside and fluffy within. Just like my mum used to make. My perfect Sunday lunch.

My parents say I fell in love with roast beef when I was just three weeks old, their first child, born in February 1967. The local health visitor arrived at our Norwich home to perform the usual post-natal checks and was apparently aghast at how big I was already. Family folklore recalls her declaring that breast milk was insufficient to satisfy the appetite of this hungry child and recommended I be moved onto 'solids' straight away. 'Just pulp him up a little of what you're eating,' she told my mum. I'd only been in the world twenty-one days and already I needed a roast dinner.

My dad drove into Norwich to buy a fancy new food

blender. The Moulinex from France had been the must-have kitchen gadget for a few years but my parents had never previously been able to justify the extravagance. It's striking now, looking back at the adverts of the time, to see how much things have changed since then. The Moulinex was presented as the next frontier for the Women's Liberation Movement to *bring the fight for freedom right into the kitchen*. Wives and mothers were still expected to do all the cooking, but this push-button blender would make things quicker, 'liberating' them to throw off their aprons and even allowing them to go out to work as well!

That weekend, my small portion of Mum's Sunday roast lunch was 'mouli-ed' to a smooth paste and I wolfed it all down. Today, the health advice is no solid food for at least the first six months. What can I say? We lived by different rules back then.

Sunday roast dinner remained the most important meal of the week when I was growing up, part of a fixed routine that you could set your clock by. My mum went to the butcher's on Saturday morning – we had beef, pork or lamb in weekly rotation, chicken less often, and always with Yorkshire puddings. She would set the oven timer before we drove off to church on Sunday morning and when we returned home, around half past twelve, the smell of roasting meat was already creeping under the kitchen door, enveloping us like a huge fuggy blanket as we walked into the house. My parents always had a glass of sweet sherry, my dad carved the meat and we had the BBC's *Family*

Favourites on the radio in the background, with forces families requesting songs and sending messages to their loved ones serving around the world.

My younger sister and brother and I were expected to be sitting down at the table on time for the food to be portioned out, and there was always a hushed tension as the first of us poured the gravy over our full plates. No matter how many times we tried, for some reason there was never quite enough gravy to go round, and whoever went first had my dad watching like a hawk to make sure they didn't overpour.

I loved my mum's food, and cooking was one of the most special things she taught me. And it had to be her, because I can hardly ever remember my dad doing anything in the kitchen. He worked, gardened, carved – and ate – and my mum did the shopping, cooking, cleaning and everything else involved in looking after the family. It was her full-time job until I was eleven, and – Moulinex or no – it didn't get any easier when she also took a part-time job with the NHS.

My dad did have one foray into the kitchen on the day my brother, Andrew, was born in 1973. He stayed at home to look after me and my sister, Joanna, and cooked roast beef and Yorkshire puddings, which were so good that we took a pudding into the maternity hospital that evening for our mum to eat. Dad declared it a triumph and promptly retired, never to cook again until my mum's dementia turned their lives upside down.

Now, when my brother and sister and our families get

together with my dad, and my mum visits from her nearby care home, it has become my job to cook the roast beef and Yorkshire puddings the way Mum taught me, making sure all the kids are sitting down in good time, and keeping a close eye on the gravy boat as it journeys round the table.

Sunday roast is an important family tradition, but it's also one I love to share. The night before the general election in 2015, when I lost my seat and my political career suddenly ended, I cooked roast beef for all my exhausted campaign team with twenty-four Yorkshire puddings, just enough for one each. When I was eliminated from *Strictly Come Dancing* the following year and invited my partner Katya over with her husband Neil, I chose roast beef to welcome them into our family, while their tiny dog Crumble yapped around our feet.

And when our intrepid team climbed high into the African clouds, scaling Kilimanjaro for Comic Relief in 2019, I reminisced with Jade Thirlwall from Little Mix and *Love Island*'s Dani Dyer about roast dinners and family Sundays at home as we trudged along, a memory just as warming and comforting for them in their twenties as for me in my fifties. We agreed that when we got down, and could all gather again back home, I would cook roast beef and Yorkshire puddings for the team. And I did – easily the most glamorous back garden gathering our family has ever seen.

Little did I imagine then that those kinds of meals with friends would become impossible just a year later in 2020.

Most painfully, our cherished family get-togethers with Mum and Dad in Norwich were put on hold. In lockdown, when so many of us had our immediate family thrust together for months at a time but were forced apart from our wider family and friends, I came to appreciate how important food, recipes and the ritual of a meal can be to our collective sanity and wellbeing.

It reminded me how important the combination of food, family and love has been throughout my life, a constant comfort in our changing world, and one which I've been lucky to experience in the kitchen as well as round the dinner table, as a dad as well as a son.

I'm a cook who loves to experiment, but there are some tried and tested recipes that have featured in my life so regularly that they have come to take on their own identity, irrevocably linked in my mind with the times I've spent around the table with the people I love. What were once just recipes wheeled out for casual meals have taken on a new significance as I've got older; as my kids have started to embark on their own adult lives, and my parents have become our guests rather than hosts, we are still connected by the food we love. This is a collection of the meals I love to cook most, and the memories they bring back, from childhood to Westminster to parenting. The world might have changed since 1967, but the best recipes last a lifetime.

ROAST BEEF WITH YORKSHIRE PUDDINGS

Serves 5

This is my favourite meal in the world, the most important recipe my mum taught me and one I have used again and again. It needs roast potatoes, parsnips, carrots and lots of green vegetables. There will definitely be leftovers: cold meat to eat on Monday with pickles; spare gravy to make a rich shepherd's pie; and, best of all, potato and vegetables to be mashed up with salt, pepper and a beaten egg and fried in patties in a pan or baked in the oven to make lovely bubble-and-squeak.

Ingredients

- 1kg beef joint (I always go for unrolled sirloin, but topside is also fine)
- 1 tbsp Dijon mustard
- Salt and pepper
- 1 tbsp plain flour
- Slug of red wine (optional)
- 450ml beef stock (I always try to use liquid stock – chicken stock is also fine and makes a lighter gravy – or use the vegetable cooking water if you don't have any stock)

For the Yorkshire puddings

- 85g plain flour
- Pinch of salt
- 2 eggs
- Dash of water
- 140ml whole milk
- Vegetable or groundnut oil

For the roast potatoes

- 8 large potatoes, peeled and halved
- 4 tbsp olive oil
- Salt and pepper

Method

1. Put the potatoes (and parsnips if you want) in salted water, bring to the boil and simmer for 10 minutes before draining.

2. Make the Yorkshire puddings: put the flour in a bowl with the salt and whisk in the eggs and the dash of water; then slowly beat in the milk to form a batter – I usually make the batter a couple of hours in advance, but last minute will also work. Cover and set aside. Turn the oven on to 220°C/425°F/gas mark 7. Drizzle the olive oil in a baking tray and put in the oven to heat up.

3. Salt the bottom of the joint and place into a roasting pan. Smear the mustard over the fat and season generously. Put into the hot oven and cook for 25 minutes. Then turn the heat down to 180°C/350°F/gas mark 4 and cook for a further 25 minutes for pink, 35 minutes for medium, or 45 minutes for well done.

4. At the same time, tip the par-boiled potatoes into the hot, oiled baking tray, season with salt and pepper and cook for 50 minutes – the same time as the meat if going for pink. (If you are cooking the meat for longer, simply put the potatoes in a little later.)

5. Pour a dash of vegetable or groundnut oil into the individual indents of the pudding tin, then put it in the oven. When the meat is done and taken out, turn the oven up to 230°C/450°F/gas mark 8. The meat and roast potatoes

should be taken out of their roasting tins and rested, covered in tin foil.

6. When the pudding oil is hot, pour off any excess oil – it should sizzle if you splash a drop of water on the tin – and divide the batter equally. Cook the puddings in the oven for 15 minutes, making sure not to open the door before then.

7. While the puddings are in the oven, cook the vegetables, add a tablespoon of flour to the meat tin and put it back on the heat. When it starts to sizzle, add the red wine (if using) and stir. After 30 seconds, add the stock, stir to get rid of the lumps and leave to simmer and thicken. Carve the meat into slices, pouring the juices back into the gravy. You can always add a bit of water from the vegetables if you need more gravy, and add salt and pepper if needed.

1

GROWING UP

I started school in 1972. Every morning, from the age of
five onwards, I would wave to my mum as she stood at
the window and walk with my friends down our road,
over the main village street, and down School Lane to
the playground of our small primary school. I can barely
remember any of the seventy pupils being walked to school
by their parents.

In the holidays and at weekends, I would head off every
morning to play with my friends in the fields around the
next-door farm. We'd go back home for lunch and then
head out again all afternoon for another round of Hide and
Seek. None of our parents ever knew where we were and
never seemed to worry as long as we came home in time
for dinner or when we were hungry, whichever was sooner.

The food at Bawburgh School was good and stodgy,
cooked in the small kitchen. It's appalling to recall now, but
my friends on free school meals were made to stand at the
back of the line and wait till everyone else had been served.

At morning break, we each had our mandatory small bottle of government-provided milk. In the cold winter of 1973, the milk was often frozen – as were we, sitting in our classrooms in coats and jumpers. The miners' strike and the Three-Day Week meant we had no heating, but school carried on as usual.

The UK had moved over to 'new money' in 1971 and we got used to measuring our purchases at the local village shop in pennies. A can of coke cost 5½p, a bag of crisps 3p, while a penny could buy you eight 'fruit salads'. The chewing gum machine outside only took 2p coins, which seemed extortionate, even for the pleasure of turning the handle and hearing the pack of gum drop down in the machine.

Comics were a much more extravagant purchase, which is why we pored over every story and cartoon they contained. Later, after we moved to Nottingham in 1975, I went down to the local newsagents every Saturday with my 50p pocket money to buy a copy of *Tiger & Scorcher* or *Roy of the Rovers*, a quarter of pear drops or pineapple chunks, and put the 20p left over into my Post Office account to save for Christmas presents.

Our house in Norfolk had a telephone, but it was a 'party line' with our neighbour two doors down, so if you picked up the receiver and Mrs Hindle was on the phone, you had to hang up and wait for her to finish. We had a black-and-white television – it wasn't until we moved to Nottingham in 1975 that we could watch telly in colour. For children like us, it was the era of *Tiswas* and *Multi-Coloured Swap*

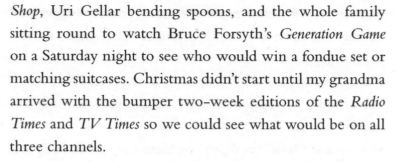

Shop, Uri Gellar bending spoons, and the whole family sitting round to watch Bruce Forsyth's *Generation Game* on a Saturday night to see who would win a fondue set or matching suitcases. Christmas didn't start until my grandma arrived with the bumper two-week editions of the *Radio Times* and *TV Times* so we could see what would be on all three channels.

There was an order and ritual about almost everything in life: the milkman delivering two pints every morning; the man coming round every week to collect the money for my dad's football pools; and a lorry driving down our close once a fortnight delivering bottles of fizzy pop – lemonade, cherryade, cream soda or dandelion and burdock – and collecting the empties.

In that world and at that young age, my cousin Frances seemed like the most glamorous person imaginable. She was ten years older than me, wore all the latest trends, and – most exciting of all – had a Saturday job at the Wimpy in Sheringham. When we went to visit my uncle and aunt up on the north Norfolk coast, Frances would entertain me, my sister and brother for hours, talking us through the menu she'd serve at weekends.

We swooned over her vivid descriptions of huge banana splits slathered with cream and sprinkles, Brown Derbies dripping with chocolate sauce and knickerbocker glories in glasses so big you needed an extra-long spoon to reach the tinned strawberries at the bottom. We watched Frances leave for her shift on a Saturday, dressed in her brown uniform and flat shoes, and in our dreams, we went with her, agonising over whether or not to have cheese on our hamburgers, and which dessert we'd choose.

But that's where it stayed — in our dreams. We went to Sheringham every year for our holiday to look after the house and dog — and sometimes Frances — when Auntie Doreen and Uncle Frank, the local Barclays Bank manager, went off for their allotted fortnight in a Portuguese time-share. We had packed lunches on the beach and freshly cooked donuts from a stall on the front. But we didn't go to the Wimpy bar or any other restaurants.

My parents thought eating out was indulgent, wasteful and not for people like us — especially since my mum, as she always reminded us, could cook just as nice a meal for half the price. Practically the only meal we ate not cooked at home was takeaway fish and chips, usually on a Friday night, wrapped in newspaper and hurried home in the car with the tangy smell of salt and vinegar wafting over the back seat.

Even on holidays, we never ate out in cafés or restaurants, certainly not at the north Norfolk coast, but nor when we travelled further afield. Our customary summer holidays in Sheringham stopped when I was ten: Frances had grown up and left home, and that meant my uncle and aunt could book their Portuguese timeshare slot outside the school holidays. But for our family back then, foreign holidays were too expensive, and we had to make do with the best that home could offer.

Instead, Mum and Dad booked holiday cottages in the wilds of England and Wales. Their idea of holiday fun was to climb up to the top of the Long Mynd in Shropshire, Scafell Pike in the Lake District or the Welsh Black Mountain, find a sheltered spot and light the Calor Gas stove. My dad would fight to keep it alight as the wind roared around us and we waited for the kettle to boil. Then Mum would pour sachets of cup-a-soup into plastic cups, the salty, lumpy liquid a relief not so much for our appetites as our freezing cold hands.

As a child, I loved those trips across Britain. Unfortunately, my dad wouldn't leave things there. While on our holidays, he had a liking for days out in the car to see what we could manage to cover between breakfast and dinner – all the Lake District lakes, all the castles of Aberdeenshire – never getting out to enjoy them but just ticking each one off the list and cracking on to the next. These trips were so boring and my little brother invariably got car sick as we swung round country lanes. But we were on a schedule with no time to spare. Lunch was eaten on the move and my dad would even lean out of the driver's seat to take his photos while still motoring along – just to have the blurred evidence of another landmark ticked off.

On those long days in the car, we yearned instead for a windy hike up a steep hill to drink something hot and powdered out of a plastic cup. Better still, we prayed for rain. Dark clouds meant that both car trips and mountain hikes were put on hold, and even if Mum and Dad felt obliged to take us on a soggy walk into the local market town to peer in the shops and buy fresh bread for lunch, just so we'd done something in the day, we would soon return to the isolation of our moor-bound holiday home. Safe and dry inside, with the fire lit in the grate, I could settle back and read a book, or indulge my eleven-year-old obsession with dice cricket.

The closest we came to actually eating inside a restaurant in the 1970s came when an American academic colleague of my dad visited London with his family for a sabbatical. My parents had got to know him before I was born when my father was teaching on the American West Coast, and kept in touch when Dad returned in 1966 to lecture at the newly opened University of East Anglia. We took our first trip ever to London on the train and the next day boarded a double-decker bus into town from Highgate with the American family. It was the mid-1970s, punk was exploding, and over the aisle from us on the top deck sat two teenagers with dyed hair and safety pins everywhere. But that wasn't our main fascination.

Dad's friend had told us that America's most famous burger chain had started opening branches in London, with double-sized hamburgers in boxes and cokes so big you could hardly carry them, so we headed to the Leicester Square branch. The queues were enormous, there were no seats to be had, and my parents would only let us have small fries and an ordinary cheeseburger. But I did see, up close, a Big Mac in its own box. McDonald's was in Britain. The future had arrived. I've had McDonald's so many times since, usually on a long car journey with the night drawing in and the kids hungry and grumpy and demanding Happy Meals from the back of the car. But I just have to taste those salty, crispy chips and the distinctively sweet, sliced gherkin muddling with the ketchup on the burger, and I'm right back in the magic of that day in Leicester Square.

I don't think our family was unusual in not eating out. Today there are restaurants and takeaways down every high street, but – other than fish and chips and greasy-spoon cafes – restaurants were much less common back then, certainly outside the big cities. And while a chain of Berni Inns was spreading across the country, serving £1 steaks with chips and fancy liqueur coffees, ordinary pubs rarely served any food and most didn't let children in at all.

So aside from school lunches, my early food memories all revolve around eating at home or at the houses of relatives. My dad's mum Nellie was the only grandparent of mine still alive when I was born and she lived in the same small, terraced house in central Norwich where my dad had grown up. My grandpa died when my dad was just ten years old, so Nellie had to manage on her own, getting my dad through his school days and proudly seeing him and his older brother John win places at Oxford and Cambridge. We spent many happy days in the 1970s being looked after by Grandma, playing with an old clockwork train that belonged to my dad as a child and reading his old *Rupert* annuals from the 1940s. And Grandma would always cook us shepherd's pie, made with minced beef, not lamb (so technically a cottage pie, although we never called it that), which, to this day, is the true taste of my childhood.

I don't know how she managed to make it so tasty, because the recipe was very simple. The beef mince was browned with onions and carrots and then cooked in water, with plenty of salt and pepper and perhaps half a stock cube, but no garlic – as Mum always said, 'We aren't French.' The potato top was always perfectly crisp and corrugated, yet still creamy. I've never had better to this day.

My mum grew up just a couple of streets away from my dad, but she had a very different kind of upbringing. Her dad owned the butcher's shop on the Unthank Road, and she and her six brothers and sisters lived cramped above the shop, then in a bigger house round the corner. Every day the shop was shut at lunchtime and the whole family – all nine of them – sat down for a meal. Years later, when her older brothers and sisters were working in office jobs in the city centre, they still came home to eat lunch together.

It was only ever meat from the butcher's shop at lunchtime, but my fourteen-year-old mum would be sent to fetch fish and chips for my grandfather every night of the week without fail when he got home from the pub. She never objected because it gave her a chance to bump into my dad for a chat and a bit of courting on the way back, and if that meant my grandfather's fish and chips were often cold by the time she got them home, he apparently never complained.

In our family home, first in Norwich and then

Nottingham, where we moved when I was eight, we also ate together every day. Not in the middle of the day, but at six o'clock, once everyone was home from work and school. We always had meat: the leftovers from Sunday's roast with pickles on Monday; then, during the week, sausage, egg and chips; shepherd's pie; a minced meat pie; maybe pork chops; and on Saturday evening, usually chips with rump steak or my dad's favourite, a 'mixed grill' – steak, sausage, bacon and a fried egg – followed by Angel Delight – chocolate, strawberry or butterscotch – for a special weekend treat.

Sunday was the most important day in our family, and even after the roast lunch, followed by a big portion of apple pie or blackberry and apple crumble, the ritual eating wasn't complete. I spent most Sunday afternoons playing football on the local 'rec' with the boy next door and my little brother, but we had to be back home by five o'clock for the family serial on TV and Sunday tea.

Just a few hours after we'd had lunch, my mum would wheel her small teak trolley into the living room, with sandwiches, cheese on toast or Welsh rarebit. Always a homemade sponge or fruit cake. Maybe rock buns or jam tarts. But most important, the centrepiece of the trolley: tinned fruit with evaporated milk. Normally peaches, sometimes pears, and on special occasions, pineapple chunks or mixed fruit cocktail. All doused in thin, sweet, tinned milk, and regarded by all of us as the biggest treat.

This may sound odd – there was plenty of fresh fruit in the shops in those days, and I took an apple, pear or banana to school every day. But for my parents – both born in 1938 and brought up during the rationing of the Second World War and its aftermath, when fresh fruit was just not available – tinned fruit remained the height of luxury.

Many years later, when we all went on a big family cruise around the Mediterranean, I can remember the stress my parents felt when, having eaten breakfast, lunch and dinner, the ship's tannoy announced that the Midnight Buffet was now available. None of us was hungry. But it was there, it was free, and as far as my mum and dad were concerned, that meant it needed to be eaten. Those wartime habits died hard.

This may all sound very traditional and old-fashioned, as you might expect from a family that had lived in East Anglia for generations, but my mum's cooking also had an exotic twist. When my parents got married in 1961, my dad's scientific work had first taken them to Switzerland, before two years in the mid-1960s teaching in Berkeley, California and Portland, Oregon.

Those years had a huge influence on them. Politically, they saw racial injustice and student unrest at first hand, with the civil rights movement at its pinnacle, and the early protests against the Vietnam War beginning to grow. Musically, my earliest memories are of my mum singing along to the political anthems popularised by Pete Seeger – 'We Shall Overcome', 'Little Boxes', and 'Which Side Are You On?', as well as Peter, Paul and Mary and The Seekers.

The other consequence of their time in America was how

it changed my mum's cooking. Our daily and Sunday dinners remained traditionally English, but if she was hosting guests, Mum had a whole different repertoire, learned from how friends from different backgrounds on the West Coast campuses would cater for large groups.

My earliest memories of my parents entertaining at home are when my dad's graduate students were invited round. It was my job to tour the room with a bowl of peanuts before I was sent to bed. I would listen from the stairs and hear the students marvelling at my mum's exotic American-influenced cooking. She invariably made lasagne in a sloppy, rich Italian American style. And that would be followed by apple and blackberry cobbler (like crumble but with a US-style scone on the top), or plum kuchen, a German American dessert with a rich, creamy top. If I brought school friends home, they'd be taken aback by my mum producing great bowls of bolognaise sauce with long strands of 'proper' spaghetti. For kids only used to eating 'spaghetti' out of a tin – as small hoops or letters – this was very different and much more difficult and messy to eat, but hugely popular all the same.

As relatively forward-thinking as my parents' culinary habits were, however, we still had to wait for the 1980s to arrive before we finally made it to a restaurant. My mum decided she needed a change and a new place had opened near our village, The Charde in Tollerton. We children didn't find out what was happening until, on the way home from church, all dressed up in our Sunday best, my dad suddenly turned off the main road into the Charde car park. We were told to be on our best behaviour and, aged thirteen, I was expected to set the standard for my younger brother and sister.

The main courses were a selection of roast meats – it was a Sunday after all – with big tureens of vegetables. I can remember very little about the food – it certainly wasn't a scratch on my mum's homemade roast – except for the vivid moment when we were asked to choose a starter. We could have tomato soup, prawn cocktail, or a glass of freshly squeezed orange juice. Mum and Dad didn't like prawns, and we were so used to eating Mum's tomato soup that it didn't feel like anything special, so all of us went for the orange juice, each glass served on its own individual plate with a doily and a napkin. My family, eating out at a proper restaurant. It felt like the most luxurious thing ever.

GRANDMA'S SHEPHERD'S PIE

Serves 5

The shepherd's pie that my grandma and mum cooked every week was always made with beef mince – there was no lamb in shepherd's pie in our family. But nor did we call it cottage pie – 'what's that?', we'd laugh. It remains one of my most favourite dishes to cook today, although I do spice it up a little compared to their very simple recipe: garlic softly fried with the onions, leftover gravy from the Sunday roast – beef or chicken, it doesn't matter – and if there's no spare gravy I'll use some liquid chicken stock plus a couple of tablespoons of Lea Perrin's Worcestershire Sauce to give the shepherd's pie a bit of extra tang. It's important to rough up the mashed potatoes to get a good, crispy top. As always, it's the gravy that makes the difference, both in quality and quantity – no one wants a dry shepherd's pie - so always make sure you have enough. For a vegetarian version, use Quorn mince and vegetable stock.

Ingredients

- 1 tbsp olive oil
- 3 garlic cloves, peeled and finely chopped
- 1 onion, peeled and finely chopped
- 1 carrot, peeled and diced
- 450g minced beef
- 500ml stock – liquid chicken or beef, or leftover gravy, or use a stock cube dissolved in water
- 2 tbsp Worcestershire sauce (or soy sauce)
- Salt and pepper
- 5 medium-sized potatoes, peeled and halved
- 1 tbsp butter
- 2 tbsp whole or semi-skimmed milk

Method

1. Heat the oil in a heavy pan and add the garlic, onion and carrots. Cook slowly until soft (about 5 minutes). Add the meat and, when browned, pour on the stock. Bring to the boil, add the Worcestershire sauce and salt and pepper and simmer for 25 minutes. (At this point my mum sometimes used to add half a sachet of 'chilli-con-carne' mix to make a slightly spicy version – I use two heaped teaspoons of the Cajun Spice Mix on page 137.)

2. Bring the potatoes to the boil and cook until a knife runs right through them easily. Drain and return to the saucepan. Add the butter and milk, then mash till smooth.

3. Turn the oven on to 180°C/350°F/gas mark 4.

4. Transfer the meat to an ovenproof dish, reserving most of the liquid in the saucepan to use as a gravy (you might need to strain it through a sieve).

5. Slap the potatoes on top, use a knife to smooth over and a fork to get a good texture. Cook in the oven for 30 minutes and serve with the gravy.

LAMB WITH HERBS

Serves 4

My mum always wanted a hostess trolley. When we were young, her biggest gripe on Sunday was that she couldn't keep the plates warm, and she needed a trolley like Auntie Marlene's. This fabulous contraption – which looked like a wired-up set of drawers and emitted a low hum when plugged in – would be switched on an hour before lunch by Marlene, creating a nice warm surface for the plates in the lower warming tray and heating the vegetable tureens on the top, all ready to keep everything hot once the meat was carved and the gravy boat was full.

Whether it was because Marlene had one, or that it was considered the pinnacle of 1970s domestic sophistication, or because she was actually obsessed with the plates getting cold, my mum really wanted a hostess trolley for our house. My parents did have a Teasmade in their bedroom, which woke them up every morning at 7 a.m. with a loud buzzing noise and a flashing light as the boiling water poured out into a waiting teapot for their morning cuppa in bed. And, like many other families, we had a large chest freezer in the garage, which remained largely empty once my parents discovered that buying half a pig was a false economy, as my mum didn't know how to cook most of it and my dad didn't want her to learn.

It was for the hostess trolley, however, that my mum truly pined. Which made it all the more bizarre that, when she eventually got one, long after I'd left home, it was barely used. It took so long to move the plates and dishes in and get them out again, my mum found it easier just to put them all straight on the table, like she'd always done before. Still, it was there for special occasions and to impress visiting relatives, like Auntie Marlene and Uncle Terry. And I'm aware that my mum's odd foibles have rubbed off on me. I don't like it when the family are slow coming down for Sunday dinner – 'It'll get cold!' I shout up the stairs. And I also like to keep the gravy bubbling in the meat tin until the very last minute.

All of which explains why, when it comes to entertaining, I'm always on the lookout for dishes that taste better as they cool. That's where this lovely Ottolenghi-inspired lamb recipe comes into its own. The hard work to make the marinade is all done the day before. I tend to sear the lamb cutlets and then cook them in the oven an hour or two in advance – as they rest, they get tastier and tastier.

I use individual lamb cutlets on the bone for this recipe, but you could use lamb steaks and reduce the oven cooking time by a third. The green marinade is sweet, spicy and herby and makes a great pouring sauce. I usually heat it up and pour it over at the last minute. That's what my mum would have done, I'm sure. Though, of course, if she were cooking this dish for Marlene and Terry, she would have kept the lamb cutlets warm in her hostess trolley. Because at long last she finally could.

Ingredients

- 8 lamb cutlets, on the bone

For the marinade

- 3 garlic cloves, peeled and roughly chopped
- 2cm piece of ginger, roughly chopped
- A good handful of parsley, roughly chopped
- Coriander, same again
- Mint, same again
- 3 red chillies, roughly chopped
- 2 tbsp red wine vinegar
- 3 tbsp honey or maple syrup
- 3 tbsp soy sauce
- Juice of 1 lemon
- 1 tsp salt
- 100ml groundnut oil
- 50ml water

Method

1. Place all the marinade ingredients in a food processor for 30 seconds. If you don't have one, then just chop everything up finely. Put the lamb cutlets in a deep bowl, pour over the marinade, cover with cling film and leave for at least 3 hours, but preferably overnight.

2. Turn the oven on to 190°C/375°F/gas mark 5. Heat a griddle pan until hot and sear the lamb cutlets, a few at a time, for 2 minutes on each side, shaking off any excess marinade back into the bowl before you sear. Put the seared lamb on a baking tray and cook for 8 minutes for pink, 10 minutes for medium, or 12 minutes for well done. Layer the cooked lamb on a serving dish and let it rest for at least 10 minutes, though an hour or two is fine. Meanwhile, heat the excess marinade in a saucepan and pour over the lamb before serving.

2

LEARNING TO COOK

I can't remember much about the school trips I went on as a child, but I have vivid memories of my packed lunches. Goodness knows what I learned visiting Newark museum, church and castle. But I can see and smell my ham sandwich, ready salted crisps, Club biscuit and apple, all fitted snugly in a converted margarine tub and lovingly cradled on the coach journey. As for the fateful school trip to Birdworld when I was five, I'm still scarred by the shock of opening my lunchbox to find a large lump of cling-film-wrapped Cheddar cheese with no bread. Bewildered, I self-consciously gnawed on the hunk's corners while my friends munched more conventional bread rolls filled with ham or jam. The mystery was solved when I got home and showed my mum the nibbled cheese. She promptly squealed and opened the fridge to find my carefully-wrapped sandwich still safely stored in the cool box.

For those of us who had school lunches every day, these packed lunches, mishaps aside, were a rare and special treat.

I played every year in the District Cubs' chess tournament, not because I was any *Queen's Gambit*-style wunderkind – I was rubbish actually – but because I loved taking a packed lunch on a Saturday and spending a day in the rather beery atmosphere of the Cotgrave Miners' Welfare Hall. I was willing to spend five hours on a Sunday afternoon keeping the score at Plumtree Cricket Club because it earned me a free tea. And for three years, I had a Sunday paper round, lugging a huge and heavy bag packed with colour supplements round our village streets, looking forward to the house at the top of Debdale Lane where the lady occupant always left me a piece of homemade shortbread in return for delivering her copy of *The Observer* on time.

I also spent a summer when I was twelve working every morning with a Co-op milkman who smoked forty cigarettes in the three hours we spent driving round the village making our deliveries. The same lady left him shortbread too, which he often seemed to spend a mysteriously long time collecting, while I ate a yoghurt off the cart and waited patiently. And when I spent the run-up to the festive season working at the Nottingham central sorting office, I'd never tasted a better cooked breakfast than the one they served in the staff canteen, or been so desperate for it as I was on those chilly mornings after a couple of hours sorting hundreds of Christmas cards and gift parcels.

My favourite books when I was a child all seemed to revolve around eating, too. The best adventures at the top of Enid Blyton's *Faraway Tree* happened when the magic land involved food. Her Famous Five were always eating lashings of everything. Roald Dahl's *Charlie and the Chocolate Factory* was, of course, a natural choice. But in my most treasured stories of all – Arthur Ransome's *Swallows and Amazons* adventures in the Lake District and the Suffolk flatlands – the children didn't just eat; they cooked over a campfire. And I was desperate to do the same.

I was a keen Cub Scout from the age of eight and we soon learned to cook sausages over open fires and what we called Dunkers – flour, water and salt mixed into a dough, wrapped round a stick, cooked over a campfire and eaten, hot, chewy and salty and slathered with butter.

My personal cooking journey properly began when I started experimenting in the kitchen for myself as an eleven-year-old in the school holidays, when my mum got her first job since I was born, working part-time as an NHS clerical worker at the Queen's Medical Centre in Nottingham. She had a collection of *Reader's Digest* recipe cards which she'd brought back from America, a huge edition of Mrs Beeton's famous Victorian cookbook and, of course, Delia Smith's *Complete Cookery Course*. To begin with, I tried out recipes that didn't require many ingredients, so my efforts wouldn't be discovered. Mrs Beeton's 'One Egg Invalid Omelette' was my first success. Nowadays, the idea of a bunch of recipes designed specifically for people suffering illness at home feels odd, but in the nineteenth century it was regarded literally as a lifesaver.

I started helping out more formally by putting the

potatoes on to boil or getting the vegetables ready for when my mum got home. My big cooking breakthrough came when our Scout troop organised a six-week cooking course leading to the Cook's badge. I learned to make pastry, fruit cake and a casserole with beef and brown ale; and we practised making 'Camp Pancakes' – white sliced bread smeared with jam, folded over, dipped in pancake batter and then fried on both sides in a buttery pan.

With my Cook's badge under my belt, I started to take more of a lead at our annual Scout camp, where, rain or shine, we spent ten days away in North Yorkshire cooking only on open wood fires using the ingredients our patrol was handed each day from the Camp Store. I learned to smuggle in firelighters for when the wood was damp, but also some stock cubes and marmite to give our stews and soups a lift.

At home, I moved on from peeling the potatoes to cooking some of the family's weekday meals. My mum taught me her recipes for sponge cake, blackberry and apple crumble and, most important of all, bolognaise sauce. Not only could I now make spaghetti bolognaise ready for when everyone got home from work or school, I had also learned the base sauce for my mum's lasagne. Steadily she passed on to me the recipes from her childhood and those she had learned in America and adapted for us. And I've been using them and adding to them ever since.

My mum was undoubtedly glad to have one of her children willing to learn at her side in the kitchen, because the interest certainly wasn't going to come from my younger sister or brother. Joanna is two years younger than me and never seemed to like food, or certainly not what we ate at home. On Sundays after lunch, when my brother and I went out to play football, she would often be left sat at the table for another half an hour after we'd all left, not allowed to get down until she'd finished, her roast chicken going round and round in her mouth like a slowly spinning tumble dryer.

She hated any vegetables other than peas, and categorically refused to eat them. So much so that when my mum took her to the local GP with a dry rash on her fingers and arms, the doctor declared that she had Vitamin C deficiency, otherwise known as scurvy: the disease that sailors, denied fresh fruit and vegetables when out on the oceans, had suffered and died from for hundreds of years.

My younger brother's relationship with food was at the opposite end of the spectrum, and even more challenging for my parents, thanks to one of those incidents of childhood that can shape a life. Andrew was out shopping with my mum when the butcher opened his giant fridge to expose a whole half side of beef hanging up inside. My brother promptly fainted and had to be carried from the shop. Unable to shake off the image of the cow's partial carcass, he declared himself a vegetarian, and vowed never to eat meat again.

This might not seem so unusual nowadays, but for an eleven-year-old boy in 1985, it was rare, if you'll excuse the pun. 'Meat is Murder' by The Smiths might have been in the album charts, but the image of vegetarianism was still Neil from *The Young Ones*, not something many young boys aspired to. Nevertheless, Andrew stuck to his guns, both then and ever since. He did try a few times to break the habit in his twenties – I cooked him sirloin steak, roast chicken and lasagne at his request to see if he could be tempted. He never managed to eat any of it, though, and soon gave up trying.

His sudden lurch to vegetarianism didn't come easy for my parents, especially my mum, the butcher's daughter, who couldn't understand all the fuss. And in the early weeks after the fainting incident, she made few concessions. She served Yorkshire puddings, gravy and vegetables for his Sunday lunch as usual – but with a handful of peanuts substituted for the beef.

Having helped raise and feed three kids myself, I pity my poor mum. A daughter who didn't eat vegetables and a son who didn't eat meat. I was the only one who ate everything she put in front of me, and wanted to learn how to cook it too, so no wonder she was a keen teacher.

Once I left for university and my sister was out after work in the evenings, my mum gave up trying with my brother and chose the easy way. She gave him a weekly allowance and left him to buy vegetarian ingredients or ready meals at Sainsburys on his way home from school. As a Cub and Scout himself, he was already well trained.

I was aghast on every level. Like many oldest children, I'd had to put up with parents who were strict about everything: what I ate, when I went to bed, what clothes I wore, and keeping me to the 'rules of the house', whether that meant sitting down for meals on time or not running up the phone bill chatting to friends. All that was out of the window by the time my little brother reached secondary school, and on top of that, he was doing all his own shopping and cooking – even if it was just putting vegetarian pasta bakes in the oven.

It wasn't only discipline, family meals and mandatory meat-eating that collapsed after I left home. For some reason, when I went off to university, my parents decided it was time for the family to have a dog – something they had resisted for the previous eighteen years while I was at home. But rather than dwell on the choice of my replacement, I volunteered to train the eight-week-old puppy when I came home for the Easter holidays.

And what a joy it was. Tess, a beautiful Golden Retriever named after Thomas Hardy's ill-fated heroine, immediately slotted into the family hierarchy: devoted to my mum and dad, who fed her; playful with me, who trained her; obedient to my sister, who intimidated her; and openly contemptuous towards my brother, whom she'd clearly decided was beneath her in the pecking order, responding to his every entreaty to sit, stay or come with a baleful look that said: 'Who do you think you are, then, sonny?'

Tess lived a good and long life and my parents have had Golden Retrievers ever since. But Tess changed our family life in very unexpected ways. For one thing, suddenly my mum and dad were getting much more exercise than they ever did – Tess would jump up, bark and get her lead every time the *Coronation Street* or *EastEnders* theme tunes came on, demanding to be taken out. But her arrival also made my very traditional family much more demonstrative emotionally than ever before she arrived. Don't get me wrong, I come from a loving family, but we just weren't the kind to show it. Having a very huggable, kissable dog working her way round the family seemed to break down some of those barriers.

That came hardest of all for my dad, who was always the complete opposite of 'touchy-feely'. It was only when I joined *Strictly*, in my late forties, where hugging (like fake tan) is almost a religion, that I got into the habit of hugging my dad. I think he has eventually come round to it. But I can still remember the fear in his eyes the first time I moved towards him with open arms.

My dad's gradual conversion to hugging – a bit like my brother's sudden conversion to vegetarianism – is proof that none of us are set in stone in terms of who we are, and so much of our behaviour isn't really intrinsic to our personalities, so much as playing the role we think we're expected to play, at the time and in the society we happen to live in. I often think about this when people are surprised that I do the majority of the cooking in our house now. It's much more normal now for dads to do their fair share around the house, but in *my* dad's day, cooking, like hugging, was very much the mum's job.

Back in 1967, the day before my due date, my dad boarded the special train at Norwich Station to see the Third Division Canaries take on the mighty Manchester United in the fifth round of the FA Cup. Norwich won and I arrived a week late. But my dad still wasn't at the maternity unit when I was born, nor was he there for the arrival of my sister and brother. And that was far from unusual. Yvette's father wasn't there for the birth of his two oldest children, and while he was there for the third, it was despite his best efforts not to be. In those days, it was routine to be at the football on a Saturday and hear a new dad be told the news of his son or daughter's birth over the tannoy system, always accompanied by a big laugh and cheer from the crowd.

When I compared notes with Yvette about our dads, hers obviously did more cooking than mine, but mainly on special occasions. They both grew vegetables and dabbled in homemade wine, and both did odd jobs around the house – actually, Yvette's dad built a whole kitchen extension, although it took him over ten years; my dad only managed a lean-to greenhouse, but he did get it done over two weekends. There was no expectation that they would do any of the day-to-day chores involved in running a home, though: the constant round of cooking, cleaning and washing. Paternity leave was an unknown concept.

My life as a dad has been hugely different. I was there for the birth of all our children and I'd already done more cooking at the end of the first week of our first daughter's life than my dad ever did when any of us were at home. Since then, I've shopped and cooked for our family throughout our children's lives, partly because I enjoyed it, and partly because Yvette clearly didn't. But I'm certainly not unusual. As our society has changed, as many more women have gone out to work and shift patterns have become more complex, these days many more dads and grandads will pick up the kids from school, take them home and make their tea.

There are aspects of my parenting where I have consciously departed from the way I was brought up. Being more demonstrative, for a start. And trying to be more understanding and accepting of our children and their desire to do things differently. And yet, as I've got older, I see so many similarities and echoes of my parents in how we live our lives. Looking at old family photos of my dad with his two older brothers – broad, stocky and smiling – I see me and my brother today and how we'll grow old too.

Often when I stand in the street and gawp at a passer-by wearing ridiculous hipster clothes, or riding a three-wheeler bike, Yvette will say, 'Stop staring, you're just like your mother.' As Yvette and I mellow with age, and go soft on our youngest daughter, I can only smile at the annoyance of our two older kids, who complain that they got the strict end of the stick, just as I did about Andrew getting it easy all those years ago. And when we now sit down for Sunday lunch and I watch nervously as the first person pours gravy from the boat – 'not too much, it's got to go round' – I could be at home, aged seven, hearing my dad say the same.

Our parents shape who we are to such a great extent and, as I get older, I see that more and more. So, for our children now moving into adulthood, people of their own, with different interests, careers and perhaps in time different approaches to parenting, too, I celebrate those differences, but I also know deep down – or at least hope – that they won't truly break away, and, like me and my parents, they'll be glad that they didn't.

SPAGHETTI BOLOGNAISE

Serves 5

Spaghetti bolognaise has been a staple throughout our kids' childhood, just as it was through mine, and it still owes its origins to the recipe my mum taught me back in Nottingham. For our children, I would often cook a bolognaise sauce at the weekend and leave it in the fridge for the week ahead. Then my mother-in-law, Grandma June, would turn up with another one ready-made for Monday night. I reckon they sometimes had it three times a week, and our youngest daughter would have eaten it every day if she could. On holidays, she often did.

Dried oregano and lots of tomato purée are the key ingredients in this rich and tomatoey sauce, plus good stock. And this recipe is also very versatile: it is the meat base for lasagne and, with a few strategic additions and subtractions, it becomes a good and spicy chilli (I've added those changes here too). You can always use Quorn mince and vegetable stock to make it vegetarian.

Ingredients

- 2 tbsp olive oil
- 3 garlic cloves, peeled and finely chopped
- 1 large onion, peeled and finely chopped
- 1½ medium carrots, diced
- 450g minced beef
- 400g tin of peeled plum tomatoes
- 500ml chicken stock
- 400ml water (to fill the tomato can)
- ½ tube tomato purée
- 1 tbsp dried oregano
- ½ tsp salt
- ½ tsp black pepper
- 300g spaghetti
- Cheddar cheese (or Parmesan), grated

Method

1. Heat the olive oil in a wok or heavy pan and, when sizzling, add the garlic, onion and carrot and cook for 5 minutes until soft and starting to brown. Add the beef and stir until it has all browned and any lumps have been broken down. Roughly chop up the tomatoes before adding them to the meat, followed by the stock and water. Squeeze in

the tomato purée and add oregano, salt and pepper. Bring to the boil and then simmer for 30 minutes until nicely thickened.

2. Put the spaghetti into a large saucepan, add boiling water and cook according to instructions. When it's done (it should stick if thrown at a wall, or just bite it), drain and rinse with cold water, ladle the spaghetti into individual bowls and serve with bolognaise sauce and sprinkled with cheese.

Chilli con Carne Variation

To make a really good chilli con carne, these are the small changes you need to make to the bolognaise recipe above:

Additions

- 1 stick of celery, diced
- 400ml tin of kidney beans, drained
- 1 tsp ground cumin
- 1 tsp cayenne pepper
- 1 tsp paprika
- 1 tsp chilli powder
- ½ tsp ground cinnamon
- 1 bay leaf

Method variation

1. Add the celery in when you cook the onions, garlic and carrots.
2. Reduce the amount of tomato purée to 3 tablespoons, and at the same time add the remaining additional ingredients.
3. Simmer for at least an hour and a half, adding some more water if needed.

APPLE & BLACKBERRY CRUMBLE

Serves 6

I've never been a big custard fan. I was too scarred by the stodgy gloop we got served for school dinners. I love custard cold in a trifle and I like the way it cools on an apple crumble and becomes sticky and chewy. But poured, lumpy and hot, over a chocolate sponge or jam roly poly? No thanks. Given the choice, I would always much rather have double cream – and of course my mum and dad would choose evaporated milk every time. Yvette, on the other hand, always wants custard, and I'm often in trouble for forgetting to make it, although frankly, while she says she likes my homemade custard, she'd be just as happy with Bird's Instant.

Whether you prefer custard or cream, there is no better dessert to pour it all over than a crumble or cobbler. I love crumble, with a spoonful of double cream added after you've rubbed together the flour, butter and sugar to give the topping an extra richness. I think a cobbler is even better, though, with the same fruit base as a crumble but with a lighter, scone-like topping. It's one of the recipes that my mum brought back from America.

My mum reckoned blackberry and apple is the ideal fruit combination, but there are lots of variations. You can easily miss out the blackberries or vary the spices to exclude cinnamon or substitute nutmeg. If you change the fruit, you will need to vary the preparation a little, however. If using rhubarb or plums, cut into 2cm pieces, sprinkle with sugar and bake in the oven at 170°C/325°F/gas mark 3 for 20 minutes. If using gooseberries, cook in a saucepan but without the butter and spices and twice the sugar – caster sugar might be better than brown. Both crumble and cobbler absorb cream or custard, so I've included my custard recipe just in case (which is much better than Bird's if you ask me).

INGREDIENTS

- 4 large Bramley apples, peeled, cored and quartered
- 2 tbsp butter
- 2 tbsp dark brown sugar
- ½ tsp cinnamon
- 150g blackberries

FOR THE CRUMBLE TOPPING

- 250g plain flour
- 125g unsalted butter
- 50g dark brown sugar
- 50g caster sugar
- 1 tsp mixed spice
- 1 large dollop of double cream

For the cobbler topping

- 140g butter
- 280g plain flour
- 140g caster sugar
- 1 egg
- 100ml whole milk
- ½ tsp cinnamon
- ½ tsp baking powder
- 2 tbsp demerara sugar

For the custard

- 400ml whole milk
- 3 egg yolks
- 2 tbsp caster sugar
- 1 tbsp cornflour
- 1 tsp vanilla essence

Method

1. Put the apples in a saucepan with the butter, sugar and cinnamon and cook on a moderate heat for 15 minutes. The apples should be softening but not collapsing. Transfer to an ovenproof dish and sprinkle the blackberries over them.

2. Preheat the oven to 180°C/350°F/gas mark 4.

FOR THE CRUMBLE

In a large bowl, rub the butter into the flour until it resembles fine breadcrumbs. Mix in the sugar and mixed spice, followed by a large spoonful of double cream. Spread the crumble mixture over the fruit and bake for 30 minutes.

FOR THE COBBLER

Rub the butter into the flour until you have light breadcrumbs. Add the sugar, cinnamon and baking powder. Whisk the egg into the milk and add to the dry ingredients. Combine until you have a soft scone mix. Form the mixture into eight balls, flatten and lay over the fruit. Sprinkle with demerara sugar and cook for 30 minutes until golden brown.

FOR THE CUSTARD

1. Put the milk on and slowly bring it to the boil. Meanwhile, mix the egg yolks, sugar and cornflour until it resembles a yellow paste.
2. When the milk is hot but not quite boiling, take it off the heat and pour roughly a quarter of it onto the paste, mix quickly with a wooden spoon and return the smooth mixture to the milk pan.
3. Return the milk to the heat and stir to thicken, making sure the milk doesn't boil. Take off the heat and pour into a jug.

3

COOKING TO IMPRESS

'I'm not sure you're quite appreciating what a big deal this is,' my new girlfriend Yvette told me, a little sharply. It was April 1994 and we were driving down to her parents' house for my first-ever meeting with her mum, June. 'She's going to cook you a chicken curry,' Yvette continued. I was pleased, but a bit confused. After all, isn't that normal behaviour – to cook a meal when your offspring brings a new partner round for the first time?

But, as Yvette went on to explain, there was rather more to it than that. Apparently, her mum had taken the rather drastic step of retiring from doing any cooking at all when Yvette's younger brother had left home the year before. After twenty years of slaving in the kitchen, June had decided enough was enough. But she was making an exception: her daughter was bringing home a new boy-friend, and she was taking out the apron again to cook for me. At the time I was honoured by the significance of the moment, but, in retrospect, I was missing the warning signs.

Like mother, like daughter – this was a sure indication of things to come, or rather things *not* to come, where Yvette's cooking was eventually concerned.

Yvette and I had met a couple of times through mutual friends, but we only got to know each other properly when I left the *Financial Times* in 1994 to work for Gordon Brown, the then shadow chancellor. Yvette was already working for Harriet Harman, then Gordon's deputy as shadow chief secretary, but only part-time while she continued to recover from a year-long debilitating bout of ME. I was assigned to share a small office with Yvette in a Parliament building on Millbank. I'm not sure to this day whether us being paired together was something Harriet and Yvette had managed to engineer, either to spy on Gordon's new adviser, or to set the two of us up. The only thing I'm sure about was that Gordon himself had nothing to do with it. He possesses many great abilities, but I doubt very much that match-making is one of them.

Regardless of the reasons we came together, however, from the beginning we got on very well. And after just a couple of months we had what I guess you would now call our 'first date' – watching a film at my flat in Dalston, East London. We drove down the Embankment that evening in my Renault 5 automatic, singing raucously to Elvis Presley's 'Can't Help Falling in Love' – 'Take my hand, take my whole life too' – which four years later we had the whole congregation sing at our wedding. And as we drove into Hackney, we stopped at the best local fish shop, Faulkners, and bought cod and chips twice, both with mushy peas, to take back to my flat.

Yvette soon raised the stakes on the food front, taking me to a Japanese restaurant. I'd eaten sushi before in Tokyo, when I was working there for the *FT*, but never before in the UK, so this was the height of exotic dining. Jin Kichi had great sashimi, and diners could sit upstairs around the yakitori bar, watching the chef barbecuing and enjoying the smells of smoky mackerel and sweet and salty chicken caramelising over the coals. We had beer and warm sake and lots of raw fish dipped in soy sauce and wasabi, and it became a favourite place.

But we didn't cook for each other to begin with. Yvette had lived on pasta and bacon sandwiches when she was laid low with her illness, and for me, cooking had gone on the back burner since I'd left home. Being elected student president meant I lived in college accommodation all three years, with no proper kitchen to work in; and from Oxford I went straight off on a scholarship to Harvard's Kennedy School of Government. It was my first trip to America, and my first-ever flight on an aeroplane. This was the world before emails and the internet, and calling home was hugely expensive so I had to make do with a 10-minute phone call once a week. While I was there, I should have taken a leaf out of my mum's book and expanded my culinary range. But the reality was the enormous choice of great, cheap restaurants and diners in Cambridge, Massachusetts – Mexican, BBQ, Chinese, pizza – made cooking unnecessary. I made up for lost time in my youth and ate out as much as possible instead.

With my Harvard graduate degree complete, I then travelled with my English friend, Murray, on an enormous summer car journey – Boston, New Orleans, Los Angeles, Vancouver, Salt Lake City and back to Boston. We saw the July 4th fireworks in Washington DC and came dangerously off the road late at night in Mississippi after dinner at a roadside BBQ shack. We were stranded for days in Louisiana with car trouble, which we spent slurping thick Cajun gumbo soup, eating sugary donuts and listening to daytime jazz. We saw the oldest house in America in Santa Fe, said to be built in 1495, marvelled at Disneyworld in LA and camped in Yellowstone where we had a close shave with a bear. And we ate in amazing roadside diners across the continent, usually massive breakfasts of bacon, pancakes, eggs and grits. One evening we stopped at a chicken chain place on the way into Atlanta. 'Are you boys foreign?' the waitress asked us, hearing our accents. 'Let me guess. Are you from Massachusetts?' Even more foreign than that, we replied.

Nor did I do a lot of cooking when I returned from America to work, aged twenty-three, as a leader writer at the *FT*. First sharing a flat and then living alone in East London, I continued eating out a lot. Hackney had recently seen big influxes of Kurdish, Turkish and Cypriot refugees to add to the big Caribbean and Jewish communities from previous generations. As well as many new travel agents and neon-lit basement clubs, we benefitted from the rapid expansion of late-night Turkish food joints – not just kebab shops, but smoking ocakbasi grills and fancier restaurants. They all stayed open until 3 or 4 in the morning and served sumptuous grilled chicken and lamb, börek pastries and soft, flat bread. Mangal and Istanbul Iskembecisi were my favourite places.

Linking up with my friends Tom and Brigit, who lived in the flat above, we held parties that went on even later into the night than the Turkish restaurants, and where multiple hosts meant random guests arriving at all hours. The 1 a.m. arrival of Evan Davis at one party, now the distinguished presenter of BBC Radio 4's *PM* programme, decked out in leather and extensive chains is an image I will never forget.

Within six months of us sharing an office, Yvette and I were sharing that flat in Dalston. Over the next couple of years, we indulged our mutual love of the Little Chef Olympic breakfast and expanded our range of cafes, pubs and restaurants: experimenting with Swedish (smoky cured fish and aquavit); Vietnamese (super fresh and tasty beef and prawn spring rolls); and Thai (rich and fiery green and red chicken curry) – all dishes that went in my mental recipe book, and that still remind me of the early years of our relationship when I eat them.

When Yvette moved in, our home cooking took off. She was working at the *Independent* newspaper in Canary Wharf and would pop into the little Tesco next to her office and buy things to cook that evening. Our inspiration was *The 30-Minute Cookbook*, newly published that year by the *Observer* journalist Nigel Slater. He was one of a new wave of celebrity chefs who focused less on teaching technique, like Mrs Beeton and Delia Smith's invaluable *How to Cook*, and more on easy, day-to-day cooking but with more exotic ingredients. His recipes were tasty and simple, designed for busy working people like us, and perfect for developing new specialties.

Yvette became a dab hand at mushroom risotto and Italian bean salad. I experimented with stir-fries and simple Thai curries. We made sauces and marinades for sausages, pork and lamb chops. My favourite Nigel Slater-inspired creation was grilled chicken with mustard and herbs – chicken marinaded for half an hour in a tangy mixture of red wine vinegar, Dijon mustard, olive oil, salt and pepper with some fresh tarragon or coriander, and then cooked on a griddle pan.

This was all a big change in my cooking style. The dishes I had learned from Mum had always been very straightforward. One hangover from war rationing was a deep distrust of mystery stews and sauces, when leftovers of different ingredients would be thrown together to form some type of substantial meal. After growing up on a diet like that out of necessity, my dad liked his meat, potatoes and vegetables to be easily identified and separated on the plate, with any gravy poured over them himself so he knew exactly what he was eating.

By contrast, throwing loads of ingredients together was the essence of the Slater style, and I loved the way his recipes transformed a simple pork chop or chicken breast by injecting new flavours like chillies, lemongrass, coriander and limes which I had never used before. As cooking fashion changed, so too did the kind of food you could buy at the supermarket. In the 1990s, celebrity chefs with cooking shows – Delia, Nigella, Rick Stein, Gary Rhodes – were now cooking recipes using more exotic ingredients, which the supermarkets were able to source from around the world much more easily. We could soon buy fresh herbs and fancy ingredients that just weren't available to our parents' generation, even after rationing had ended.

Yvette and I cooked for each other, but also for friends at the weekend. We became more adventurous, serving up our version of new tastes we had tried in restaurants – fresh Vietnamese spring rolls, sesame prawn toast – but also dishes I had sampled on my travels in America and at the *FT*: Cajun jambalaya, spicy quesadillas and sweet, yam-packed Ghanaian peanut stew. One Friday morning we woke up to a terrible stench at 5 a.m. to realise that I'd forgotten to turn off the chicken stock pot that I'd got going the night before. The smell lasted well over a week.

A year later we set up a joint account to start saving for a deposit, and shortly afterwards decided to take an even deeper plunge by inviting both sets of parents round to meet each other. We waited until my mum and dad would be over visiting from Italy, where Dad had become head of a European Commission research centre, and, in their honour, we cooked lasagne using my mum's recipe. The stress was incredible as we waited for them all to turn up. Would our mums get on? Would our dads argue about politics? Was the food going to be up to scratch? And would the flat be clean enough to pass my mum's inspection? During dinner itself, we were so tense that Yvette and I packed, ran and then unpacked the dishwasher three separate times – just for something to do, to avoid having to sit at the table and deal with the embarrassment.

But of course, our parents weren't embarrassed at all. They tucked into the food and wine and got on like a house on fire. In fact, they all drank much too much. At one point, my dad was sitting on the back of the sofa regaling everyone with some long story about European bureaucracy when he lost his balance, fell backwards over the sofa and did a full backward roll onto the floor. He didn't stop talking during his tumble, however, or even let go of his – now empty – wine glass. Yvette's parents didn't bat an eyelid.

My mum adored living in Italy, learning the language and the new cuisine, even if my dad's deeply inconvenient dislike of pasta made things challenging. Yvette and I visited regularly and loved the Italian bread, which you had to buy daily as it quickly went stale, and the fresh pasta which I didn't know even existed – I just assumed it always came dried. Every Sunday, however, even in the baking Italian sun, my mum still cooked a Sunday roast. That became Yvette's first experience of my mum's cooking, and given our preference for a pinker, juicier slice of beef, Yvette struggled to get through it. 'It's a bit well done,' she whispered to me when my parents were in the kitchen. But she did agree the gravy was good.

Italy became our automatic summer holiday of choice. We could have flown out to Milan. But why make it easy? Yvette and I instead regularly drove down through France to Italy in my small Renault 5. On one occasion, we tried camping, but Yvette only managed an hour before declaring that she was too uncomfortable and went to sleep in the car instead. And that was that.

We also regularly visited Yvette's parents, where, with Yvette's mum in culinary retirement, her dad had been forced to take on all the cooking. It quickly became clear he was also a very good 'event cook' – his menus took weeks to prepare and his Christmas meals grew ever more complex. I was deeply impressed and learned a lot from watching him, although sometimes the complexity became a bit too much even for him. One Christmas Day, his five-course meal included a cheese sorbet – not two words I'd previously put together. But Tony had clearly put a lot of thought into it, making the concoction weeks beforehand, storing it in an ice-cream tub, and serving it fresh from the freezer in champagne glasses. It was truly disgusting and, much as all of us round the table tried, we couldn't hide the horror of each mouthful. Thankfully, Tony eventually tasted it himself, instantly removed all our glasses, went back to the freezer and returned with a full tub of the sorbet he had intended to serve, which, while a little odd, did taste as a cheese sorbet probably should. Goodness knows what we ate the first time round – it's still a mystery.

The following February, with the general election looming, Yvette organised a family party for my thirtieth birthday. The menu was sausages and mash and, on the spur of the moment, I decided to hint at a proposal in my thank-you speech. But it was already getting late and I managed to be so subtle with my phrasing that none of the twenty-five people there understood what I was saying, least of all Yvette who just stood up and said it was time for dessert.

A couple of months later, with the *Yorkshire Post* having written a profile of the newly elected MP for Pontefract and Castleford in which I was labelled her 'current boyfriend' – which made me rather grumpy at the time – we decided we had better get engaged. We were married in Eastbourne in January 1998, in a seafront hotel that Yvette's dad often used for trade union conferences. We organised a bouncy castle, a magician and the seaside novelty train to do afternoon rides and, rather than have a sit-down meal, we had evening stalls serving fish and chips (of course) plus lamb curry and lots of desserts. Bacon sandwiches were served at midnight, and all our friends with small children declared it was the best wedding their kids had ever been to.

When I think back to that very child-friendly wedding, I can see now that our biological clocks were ticking loudly. Having kids wasn't something Yvette and I had talked much about. I think we probably just assumed we would stay together and, both being from families of three, eventually have three children. And we had been in training.

Tom and Brigit from the upstairs flat in Dalston had a little girl called Rose in 1992 and I was honoured to be asked to be one of her godparents. She started nursery school just up the road from where we lived, and when her parents both needed to go to work early, they would drop three-year-old Rose off with Yvette and me in the flat below so we could take her to nursery when we were ready to leave.

One weekend, with Tom and Brigit away at a distinctly non-child-friendly wedding, Yvette and I offered to spend the whole Saturday babysitting. We went to the zoo and passed the morning looking at tigers, snakes and elephants – but I suspected if my god-daughter was anything like me as a child, she'd be most interested in lunch. At the café clutching our trays, I tried to put Rose at ease with her Uncle Ed by ignoring all the fancy options on the menu and ordering the kids' option – sausage, chips and peas – for Yvette and me and asking Rose if she'd like the same. 'No,' she replied after giving it great thought, 'I'll have the aubergine pasta bake' . . .

CHICKEN WITH
MUSTARD & HERBS

Serves 5

This midweek chicken dish is quick, easy and very tasty. It's good with green vegetables, or you could put it in a sandwich with mayonnaise and tomato. You don't need to make the sauce if you don't want to – I usually just pour all the marinade in the pan with the chicken and let it bubble. It also works well cooked under the grill. I generally use coriander, but parsley or tarragon work just as well.

Ingredients

- 4 chicken breasts, cut into quarters
- 6 tbsp olive oil
- 2 tbsp Dijon mustard
- 4 tbsp red wine vinegar
- A good handful of finely chopped fresh herbs – coriander, parsley or tarragon are good
- 2 tbsp white wine (optional)

Method

1. Put the olive oil, mustard and red wine vinegar into a bowl and mix well. Add the herbs and chicken and mix. Leave for at least 30 minutes if you can.

2. Heat a griddle pan on the stove until hot. Add the chicken with the marinade (though shaking the excess off if you want to make the optional sauce below). Turn the heat down to medium and cook for about 8–10 minutes until cooked through – I usually start with big chunks of chicken and halve them in the pan during cooking. Transfer the chicken to a serving dish.

3. If you want, you can keep the pan on the heat and add a couple of tablespoons of white wine to sizzle while you scrape off the bits stuck to the pan. Then add the excess marinade, let it bubble for a minute and pour over the chicken. If you can't be bothered, though, it doesn't matter.

SPANISH OMELETTE

Serves 4

I've only been a best man once, when my friends, Tom and Brigit, were married in southern Spain. Brigit's family had retired to live in a tiny white mountain village called Casares, where she had spent a year off learning Spanish, and the whole village opened its arms wide to welcome her and all of us when we arrived for the celebrations. The speech I made, with my co-best man Murray, was very long and probably best forgotten. But it was a spectacular weekend. Tom and Brigit had timed their ceremony to coincide with the village's annual August festival, the 'Ferrier'. Each year the whole village ate, drank and danced all night for three nights running and we all joined in, filling the twin squares and all the surrounding bars.

The wedding breakfast was lovely, local Spanish food. But the culinary highlight of that weekend was a freshly cooked Spanish omelette. Tortilla Española tastes especially good in the early hours of the morning after a long night of eating, drinking and dancing. It should be simple and salty, perfect for soaking up

Spanish beer. This is the local recipe that Brigit learned in the village and taught me so I can relive that happy night.

INGREDIENTS

- 200ml olive oil
- 2 large potatoes, peeled and diced
- 6 eggs, lightly whisked
- Salt and pepper
- (Optional: 2 garlic cloves, peeled and finely chopped; 5cm of chorizo, skinned and chopped; 1 green or red pepper, de-seeded and chopped; or a few sliced mushrooms)

METHOD

1. Heat the olive oil in a wok or heavy-bottomed pan and when it's hot add the diced potatoes. Cook on a medium heat for 10 minutes or so until soft but not too brown. Remove with a slotted spoon and sit on kitchen roll to cool and drain.

2. Meanwhile, put 2 tablespoons of the oil into a big frying pan and heat (at this point, if using garlic, chorizo, peppers or mushrooms, you would fry them until soft and add them to the egg mixture). Put the potatoes into the egg mixture, mix, add salt and pepper and pour into the frying pan.

3.   This is where it is always a bit tricky. You want a medium heat and for the omelette to cook through without burning. I reckon after about 7 minutes, it's time to turn. Put a big plate over the top of the cooking tortilla – it will still be runny on top – and flip the frying pan. Slide the omelette back into the pan, tucking the sides in to make it neat. Cook for a further 4 minutes, but keep checking for burning. Then slide onto a plate or board. Eat straight away, but let the tortilla cool a little first as you open another cerveza.

4

POLITICAL EATING

'You must come round to my little flat on Saturday,' Peter
Mandelson smiled. 'We'll have some lunch and talk about
your future.' As a 26-year-old *Financial Times* journalist,
here I was, the year after Labour's shock 1992 election
defeat, being summoned by one of the party's most influ-
ential and controversial figures for a one-on-one meeting
to persuade me to give up journalism and work for Gordon
Brown and the Labour Party. It was the most exciting lunch
invitation I'd ever received.

We ate in the kitchen of his Wilmington Square flat in
central London, minutes away from Sadler's Wells Theatre
on Rosebery Avenue, where Peter was a patron. Everything
was pristine – the neat kitchen, beautiful plates, crisp nap-
kins – and the lunch was equally simple, small and exquisite:
tomato soup, crusty French bread, and a little green salad
with baby tomatoes and a lightly tossed vinaigrette.

As someone of my appetite would, I ate it all, assuming
it was the starter, but – perfect as it was – that was the full

lunch. If I was hosting someone, I'd have wanted to leave them turning down a third helping of dessert, but this was a different world, and as the years have passed, I realised that was the point. Lunch was on Peter's terms, and he used it to size me up, make a strong impression, and tell *me* what *my* future should look like.

That's what they call establishing a power dynamic, and the fact that I can remember it so vividly almost thirty years on shows he did a good job. The actual lunch we ate that day was important insofar as it communicated something about Peter's aesthetic, but beyond that, it was just a way of providing a social, informal and personal backdrop to a dialogue which, if it had taken place in his office or in a meeting room, would have felt more like a job interview.

Over the next few years, I learned that those kinds of meetings between political colleagues were often held over lunch or dinner as a deliberate means of defusing what might otherwise be tense or difficult discussions, or as a subconscious way of the host asserting their power over a guest, right down to imposing the choice of restaurant, table or wine. Indeed, what I rapidly discovered, to my immense disappointment, was that in politics, unlike the rest of my life, food is very rarely about food. Or, to be slightly less philosophical, food is everywhere in politics, and plays a crucial role in so many of its processes and interactions, but the actual enjoyment of what is on the plate is considered pretty irrelevant.

In 1994, when Tony Blair suggested that he and Gordon Brown meet at the Granita restaurant near Tony's home in

Islington to discuss how to handle the Labour leadership vacancy that arose after the tragic death of John Smith, the food was the last thing on either of their minds. A good thing in Gordon's case, since I could tell from the moment we walked in that it was not his type of place. The menu was short and Mediterranean. 'What exactly *is* polenta?' he asked me gruffly.

I made my excuses after their starters arrived and left the two of them alone, but the fact that Gordon did much more talking than eating during that fateful dinner was evidenced by the way he wolfed down a steak and chips immediately afterwards back in Westminster while giving me and others his version of the conversation. It's hard to imagine such a dinner happening these days – the two leading candidates to be the next leader of the opposition, most likely the next prime minister, sitting together in a restaurant on Islington's Upper Street working out the future. Today a picture would be on Twitter or Instagram within minutes. Back then it was an *Evening Standard* diarist, sitting two tables down, who got the scoop. Nothing in politics ever stays private.

Gordon finally agreed at that dinner to stand aside for Tony Blair in the Labour leadership contest. Tony may well have intimated that he would eventually stand down and hand over to Gordon. Gordon may even have believed him. But that wasn't the 'deal' Gordon was after that evening. He went into Granita determined to secure his own control over economic and social policy and make Tony's leadership a partnership between the two of them. That was what the press were told the next day as they staged a photograph walking together by Westminster Hall – and while this may be an unfashionable view, I do believe their partnership, turbulent as it was at times, worked considerably better for the nation than the Prime Minister-Chancellor relationships that followed. Both were hugely talented and driven and needed the challenge each provided to the other, however uncomfortable that was at times. When this kind of challenge and compromise is absent, bad decisions follow.

That Granita dinner is one very famous example of food not really being about the food in politics, but there are countless more. In the canteens and dining rooms of Parliament, food is a chance to gather with your tribe. When I first visited the Members' Dining Room after being elected in 2005, I moved towards the nearest table, but my arm was grabbed by a fellow Labour MP. 'That's for the Tories,' he said. He explained that the tables at one end were for the Conservatives, at the other end for Labour, with a middle table for the Lib Dems. If you were going to eat there, you did it as part of your political group, in your tribe, in your family. It was for bonding, not just food.

If a group of MPs wanted to get together for a more surreptitious discussion instead, perhaps about the future of their party leader, they can't just book a meeting room or all assemble in one of their living rooms, otherwise the immediate question is: 'What are you plotting?' So it's far safer simply to arrange a dinner. After all, what could be more innocuous than a group of colleagues going out for a meal to get away from Westminster and unwind from work? The problem being that this trick has now become so ubiquitous that if two or more politicians are spotted dining together anywhere outside Parliament, the assumption is that they *must* be plotting, even if they're not.

So you can see how, amid all these machinations, the food just becomes an afterthought. One of the most notorious political dinners of recent years came in 2006, when Tom Watson and a group of his fellow West Midlands MPs met in an upmarket Indian restaurant in Wolverhampton, twelve years on from the 'Granita Summit', to discuss their dissatisfaction with Tony Blair. Tony had just announced his intention to stay for another full term in power, having won a historic third general election the year before, but Tom and others felt he needed to take responsibility for the damage done by the Iraq War. The political implications of that gathering have reverberated for years. But ask any of the individuals involved in the so-called Curry House Plot what the chicken balti was like that night, and they'll struggle to remember.

The same is true of the famous 'Westminster lunches' between politicians and journalists: the traditional way that titbits of political gossip, or more substantive revelations about policy and personnel, find their way from the corridors of Whitehall and Parliament into the pages of the next day's newspapers or the headlines on the evening bulletins. I was never a huge fan of these lunches, in part because I found it very difficult to relax and talk naturally about the issues and personalities of the day while having to preface every sentence by saying whether or not what I was saying could be repeated, reported or quoted. A few times, I tried issuing a blanket injunction over the starters that 'I assume this is all off the record', but even that means a journalist can still report what you've told them, just not in the form of a quote.

If that made those lunches all much more trouble than they were worth, the other reason I wasn't a fan was that – again – the food was very rarely anything special. Whereas most high-class restaurants in London live and die by the quality of their cuisine, what Westminster restaurants trade on is largely the ability to have discreet conversations. As for the food they served, I'd usually have my mum's voice in my ear: 'I could make better than this for half the price at home.' Or, in the case of most Westminster restaurants, probably a tenth of the price.

The other bastion of Westminster eating, and the scourge of many MPs' waistlines, is the political reception. Dozens of these take place in the weeks when Parliament is in session, especially in the run-up to the summer and Christmas holidays. Some of them are hosted by individual ministers or government departments, but many more are put on by trade bodies, media outlets, parliamentary groupings and the like to bend the ear of politicians in an informal setting, and as an MP you sometimes have to attend at a rate of three or four a day in some busy weeks. These receptions are famous for their lukewarm wine, even in the depths of winter, the result of being held in the ancient facilities around Parliament where refrigeration and ice are at a premium. And if the wine is usually disappointing, the food is not normally much better, occasionally needing to be swerved entirely for health reasons where prawns and salmon are concerned.

By far the least memorable culinary experiences when I was in my early career in politics, however, tended to lie away from Westminster, in what was – for good reason – known as the 'rubber chicken circuit' of constituency dinners and local fundraisers all around the country. Usually held on a Thursday or Friday in a local village hall, function room or sports club, the guest speaker would tour the tables with the local candidate, draw the raffle, make a speech, and then head off on the long journey home before last orders at the bar. Now obviously you're not expecting a feast for the ages at an event like that – it was usually cheap, cheerful and enjoyable fare. Apart from anything, if the idea is to raise money, then the organisers don't want to defeat their own purpose with expensive catering.

Personally, I could never share that rationale because my attitude to local party gatherings was the complete opposite. In my view, you had one, perhaps two chances every year to put on a real bash to thank the volunteers who went out knocking on doors and handing out leaflets with you, the local businesses who donated raffle prizes, and other supporters who'd done their bit in recent months. Those events therefore became one of the culinary highlights of the local calendar if I had anything to do with organising them. And from 1997 onwards, I took as my inspiration – or perhaps

my springboard to reach greater heights – the unforgettable buffet we had in Yvette's constituency to celebrate our
engagement.

Victory in 1997 was a dream come true for me, the first
election of a Labour government in my adult lifetime. I
could remember the two 1974 Heath–Wilson elections:
we had a Harold Wilson poster in our window and my
dad took me out delivering leaflets in Norwich. After that,
though, it was one disappointment after another – with
Margaret Thatcher's three victories and Labour's surprise
defeat by John Major in 1992, which had a big influence on
my decision to go and work in the Treasury for Labour. At
the very beginning of the 1997 General Election campaign,
the MP for Pontefract & Castleford suddenly announced he
was standing down, and Yvette – still just twenty-eight –
decided to stand. After a whirlwind five days, Yvette won
the vote at a packed selection meeting of local Labour party
members. This young economist had taken on a group of
older, more experienced and better connected men, and
beaten them all. I spent the election campaign working in
party headquarters, but on election day, having met the
Permanent Secretary to the Treasury in Whitehall to hand
over a large pile of policy papers detailing our plans, I got
the train up to Doncaster to be with Yvette as the polls
closed nationwide and her own local victory was confirmed.

In the immediate whirlwind after the 1997 election, our
instinctive decision to get engaged seemed like par for the
course. But it did mean that, three weeks after the election,

we ended up combining Yvette's 'thank-you' party for her supporters at Castleford Civic Centre with our engagement celebration for our family and friends. Double the celebration, of course, meant double the food, and that party remains the greatest buffet I have ever seen, because – like all buffets – its quality is judged by its scale. A decent buffet is big. A good buffet is huge. But a great buffet is the size you usually only see in 1930s cartoons, with a hungry schoolboy or a slavering dog staring in at the window: gigantic pyramids of sausage rolls, pork pies, cocktail sausages, ham sandwiches and scotch eggs. Of course, there is sometimes some lettuce in the corner, a nod to healthy eating, and perhaps some cheese rolls for the vegetarians, but, fundamentally, these buffets are all about processed pork. I had rarely seen a more satisfied crowd of party-goers than that evening in Castleford, let alone all the local kids who woke up to the leftovers taken home by their parents.

The following year, we held a garden party for party members and supporters at our house to thank them for their hard work over the past year and raise some much-needed funds for the campaign coffers. My in-laws had just bought me an American-style two-chamber BBQ for my birthday, engineered just like a big steam engine. I cooked a fourteen-hour pulled pork BBQ for Yvette's constituents, using the recipes I'd picked up during my post-university years in America.

The fire was lit at 11 p.m. the night before, with a rota of party members drawn up to tend it overnight – 11 p.m.

to 2 a.m., 2 a.m. to 5 a.m., 5 a.m. to 8 a.m. – and keep the pork cooking. When I started to serve it up at lunchtime the next day with a spicy North Carolina-style sauce, some people looked aghast, and I got a few requests for ketchup, mustard or apple sauce instead. But a little taste was enough to persuade almost everyone.

Our BBQ has now been lit every year for twenty-three years of constituency garden parties. Generations of teenagers have volunteered to spend the early hours in our back garden tending the coals – the longest-serving veteran of those overnight vigils is now in her early forties. Even when the restrictions kicked in during the pandemic in 2020, we delivered the sandwiches by car to members' houses instead so they could eat their spicy pulled pork while on the garden party Zoom chat.

This was also the pulled pork BBQ I was preparing the night before our William and Kate royal wedding street party in 2011, when, while getting all the last-minute extras the evening before in Castleford's Asda, I got distracted and accidentally tweeted my own name. 'You're still trending,' our teenage fire-tenders kept reminding me that night … and all the next day. I'm still waiting for people to forget about that moment, but Ed Balls Day still comes around on Twitter every year.

Yvette's election in 1997 turned our lives upside down. Suddenly we lived in two places, two hundred miles apart, having to be in Westminster during the week and back in Yorkshire at the weekend. And our long working days, me at the Treasury, her in Parliament, meant cooking Nigel Slater recipes at home on a weekday evening went straight out of the window. While Yvette ate with her new parliamentary mates in the House of Commons as she waited for that night's votes, I just grabbed something quick when I got home – a bacon sandwich or beans on toast. Many times I woke up in the middle of the night – 2 or 3 in the morning – to find she still wasn't back. I'd sleepily ring the 24-hour House of Commons switchboard and mumble into the receiver – 'Are they still sitting?' – before turning over and going back to sleep.

I spent eight years as a Treasury adviser at the heart of government from 1997 onwards, working closely with both Gordon Brown and Tony Blair, and was promoted to be chief economic adviser to the Treasury, one of those historic formal titles that probably made most people in Westminster shrug, but which I felt very proud to ring and tell my mum and dad about on the evening it was confirmed. I loved those years at the Treasury: introducing big reforms from the national minimum wage and tax credits to independence for the Bank of England and more money for the NHS; slaving for months each year planning the UK's annual Budget; struggling with No10 to keep the Blair–Brown relationship on the rails; representing the UK in international meetings all round the world; working with hugely talented civil servants, advisers and ministers; and – vitally if you ask me – ensuring Britain didn't join the Euro. And the Treasury staff canteen was excellent too. But being an adviser wasn't enough. As I knew from watching Yvette, both locally and in Westminster, the really hard thing was to put your neck on the line in Parliament and be held accountable for your own decisions. In 2004, I was selected to be the Labour candidate for Normanton, next door to Yvette's constituency, and I went about building the kind of local operation that I'd seen first-hand for seven years with Yvette.

Fortunately, I took on a brilliant office manager and campaign organiser, Carol Moran, who reminded me of one of Yvette's organisers, the great Heather Hoaksey, both of them enormous believers in the power of food to motivate activists and keep them working at full tilt. With Carol's help, I also found a local campaign office: a small shop in the town centre, selling exotic lingerie, whose owner was willing to let us have it on a three-month lease. I couldn't quite work out the seasonality of their business, but we snapped up the property and got our activists working away with a diet of biscuits, iced buns, sausage rolls and tins of Quality Street, plus constantly brewing pots of coffee and tea.

A week into the election campaign, Carol called to inform me that she'd come in that morning and found crumbs and half-eaten food all over the office – all the telltale signs of a rat. I'm embarrassed to say my lifelong dread of rodents meant that I stayed away from the office until the problem was dealt with.

The ratcatcher put down some poison, and a couple of days later a bad smell wafted through my campaign HQ, upsetting the activists as they munched on their sausage rolls. Carol called the ratcatcher back, he located the smell and removed some wood panelling to reveal the now deceased rat, lying prostrate surrounded by uneaten Quality Streets in a comfy bed he'd made for himself of lacy bras and panties purloined from the previous owners.

I spent election day in 2005 touring round the constituency in a Mini Metro with a megaphone strapped to the roof rack, an old-fashioned way to campaign, but very good fun. At the end of the day, Yvette and I had fish and chips at home from the celebrated John's Fish and Chips in Castleford before returning to the local sports hall where both our results were announced. Yvette was comfortably re-elected, I won my seat with a majority of over 10,000 and headed back to London to start a tumultuous ten years in the political front line. And as for my temporary campaign office, it soon re-opened again after the election – this time as a tattoo parlour.

SLOW-COOKED PULLED PORK

Serves 8

This is the recipe I have used every year for Yvette's constituency Labour party BBQ. I cook pork shoulders outside over an indirect wood and charcoal fire in my big BBQ, but the oven works fine too, as long as you set it very low. The dry rub has a great aroma and the sharp and spicy vinegar-based North Carolina pouring sauce offsets the meat brilliantly. I reckon you should serve this in big white rolls – with coleslaw, sweet baked beans and watermelon on the side.

Ingredients

- 1 large, rolled pork shoulder

For the dry rub

- 3 tbsp paprika
- 1 tbsp cayenne pepper
- 2 tbsp ground cumin
- 2 tbsp chilli powder
- 2 tbsp brown sugar
- 2 tbsp salt
- 2 tbsp ground black pepper

For the North Carolina pouring sauce

- 300ml white wine vinegar
- 300ml cider vinegar
- 1 tbsp sugar
- 1 tbsp Tabasco
- 1 tbsp dried chilli flakes
- ½ tsp salt
- ½ tsp ground black pepper

METHOD

1. Preheat the oven to 170°C/325°F/gas mark 3 or light the BBQ.

2. Put all the BBQ dry rub ingredients in a bowl and mix well. Smear all over the pork shoulder, working it by hand into every gap and fold. Put the pork shoulder in a large roasting tin and place in the oven or BBQ.

3. After an hour, turn the heat down to 130°C/275°F/gas mark 1 and leave for 13 hours – discarding the fat from time to time. Don't skimp on the time because it won't be ready. It should be flaky and not need any carving.

4. Mix the pouring sauce ingredients to blend in a jug, and then relax. When the cooking time is up, put the shoulder – which should by now be burnt black and have shrunk in half – on a board and cut down the middle with a carving or bread knife. Scrape the flaky pork into a bowl – discarding the skin – and then pour on the spicy Pouring Sauce. A good slug will do the job – you can't overdo it really.

BEEF CASSEROLE

Serves 5

In a general election campaign, everyone has their vital role to play. Strategists in the campaign HQ craft the message; prime ministers and party leaders do battle in the TV debates; Cabinet members tour the country visiting marginal seats; local candidates kiss babies and attend hustings in churches and village halls; party members and supporters deliver leaflets, telephone voters or stuff envelopes. But as far as I was concerned, my most vital role the two times I stood for re-election was to cook.

After being elected for the historic and safe Labour constituency of Normanton in West Yorkshire in the 2005 election, the Boundary Commission broke up my constituency, and I became the candidate for the adjoining and marginal Morley and Outwood seat instead. The Morley party owned an old Methodist chapel with an office, a big meeting room and a kitchen, all a far cry from the exotic lingerie shop in Normanton, but a golden chance for me to bring my cooking and campaigning together.

We regularly organised campaign Saturdays, more often as the election came closer. Activists would come from across Yorkshire and beyond to deliver letters in the morning while I cooked in the kitchen. At lunchtime we'd all sit down together – ninety at a time – to eat lasagne, spaghetti bolognaise, chicken fajitas and, most popular of all, this excellent beef casserole, the perfect fuel for political activity. We were one big family, like my Mum and her siblings all those years ago, sitting down to rest and eat at lunchtime before we all went back to work.

This recipe is rich, comforting and easy to make. It's better if you can marinade the beef for twenty-four hours, but thirty minutes is better than nothing. And it's much easier if you can tie the herbs in a piece of muslin cloth to save you picking them all out individually.

Ingredients

- 800g beef chuck or skirt, cut into cubes
- 2 tbsp olive oil
- 3 rashers of bacon, diced
- ½ tsp salt
- ½ tsp ground black pepper
- 1 tbsp plain flour
- 1 tbsp soft butter

For the marinade

- 1 onion, peeled and roughly chopped
- 3 garlic cloves, peeled and roughly chopped
- 1 carrot, chopped
- ¾ bottle of red wine
- 1 sprig of thyme
- 1 sprig of rosemary
- 1 bay leaf
- 1 cinnamon stick

METHOD

1. Put the marinade ingredients into a large bowl with the beef, cover and leave for 24 hours. Then carefully separate out the beef, vegetables, herbs and liquid.

2. Put a tablespoon of olive oil into a heavy pan and, when hot, fry a third of the beef for 5 minutes to seal it. Remove with a slotted spoon and repeat, adding oil as needed.

3. Add the bacon into the same pan with the remaining hot oil, and fry for 3 minutes. Then add all the marinade vegetables, turn down the heat a little and cook for 5 minutes. Add back the beef, herbs and marinade liquid, bring back to the boil, add salt and pepper and then simmer – on the top of stove or in the oven at 180°C/350°F/gas mark 4 – for 2.5 hours, adding extra wine or water as needed. When the casserole is done, remove the lid and discard the herbs. Combine the flour and butter to form a paste, add to the casserole and cook for 5 minutes more. Check the seasoning and serve.

5

Becoming a Parent

The first twenty-five years of my professional career were largely spent behind a desk, either working on my computer or going through papers. That was even more true of the long periods over that time that I spent working in the evenings and weekends at home. Over the years, my main desk drawer has become a treasure trove stuffed full of mementoes from my adult life and work, and if I ever set fire to the kitchen during one of my more ambitious experiments with Japanese teppanyaki, I'll almost certainly try to empty that drawer into a suitcase before running for the door. If I only have time to grab one thing, however, it will definitely be the blurry image of our first baby at her twelve-week scan.

The year after we were married, Yvette called me in Washington DC, where I was with a UK Treasury delegation, to say she'd had a positive pregnancy test and we were on. I knew the right thing to do was to keep the news quiet at that early stage, but it was too exciting and

I immediately announced the news to the whole Treasury team and – thanks to my lack of volume control – the rest of the Japanese restaurant we were in.

Like many new parents-to-be, we started off by buying lots of books and studying the pictures. For me, though, it wasn't until that first scan that it all started to seem real, and suddenly very serious. There she was on the screen, a tiny blob with a pulsing heart and no other distinguishing features I could see. But she was alive, and I felt something inside me switch on at that moment which was never there before but has never turned off since.

Later, when I was the Cabinet minister responsible for children and families, the experts told me how vital it is that dads feel part of the pregnancy and get involved in the discussions – it's known that fathers can have a big influence over whether new mums breastfeed, so it's good they hear for themselves how important that is. I remembered how awkward I ended up feeling when I went along to Yvette's antenatal appointments, sitting in the corner and not being spoken to. I told the experts in my department that we needed to change that culture at the front line to get dads more involved.

Yvette, at least, was clear about one of my key roles when it came to the pregnancy: making sure that her food cravings were properly satisfied. I remembered from childhood that my mum had a craving for Cadbury's fruit and nut chocolate when pregnant. Oddly, Yvette craved taramasalata, which she – mistakenly as it turned out later – thought she wasn't allowed to eat while pregnant. She was also a big chocolate mousse fan, however, and, with raw eggs a definite no-go, I set out to find a mousse recipe in which the yolks were cooked. These days, that would take thirty seconds on the internet. But back in 1999, Google was just getting started, Twitter was still seven years away, and the BBC's website was very limited. After much manual searching in bookshops and magazines, I finally found a really good-looking option – less a mousse, more a dark, rich chocolate custard which baked in the oven until it was set. Fully compliant with all pregnancy guidelines, it was utterly delicious.

My other vital role was being in charge of hospital planning. Yvette booked in to have the baby in Pontefract Hospital. At any time, I needed to have the car available, the quickest route planned, and the hospital bag packed, all so we could ensure we'd be there in good time for Yvette to have the epidural she wanted. We did have one false alarm a few weeks before the baby was due, and my planning kicked in like it was an SAS raid. But there was nothing happening that night; the doctors were worried about mild pre-eclampsia and said they'd have to induce if we got to the due date, but let Yvette go home after a couple of days.

We spent the final days at home in Castleford, twiddling our thumbs, hoping nature would take its course, but resigned to the fact that the midwives might need to give things a final push. Yvette's parents came to stay, my younger brother arrived as well to offer moral support, and my own mum kept phoning for updates, poised to travel when things got under way. And we were all put to work. Bored of pacing up and down the garden, Yvette announced that, having finished painting a 'Miffy' mural on the new baby's bedroom wall, she wanted to paint our small sitting room. We drove down to B&Q to buy brushes, paint and turps. After about three brush strokes, however, Yvette thought better of it, handed the brushes over to her mum and my brother and returned to pacing up and down the garden.

For two full days, my mother-in-law prepared and painted walls while Andrew did the ceiling – he was the only one tall enough to reach. Stress levels mounted by the hour. On the morning of the second day, June turned to him and declared: 'It's already after 10 a.m., surely that's not too early to open a bottle of wine?' Yvette's dad, meanwhile, was despatched by his daughter to the garden centre and spent a happy forty-eight hours on his return planting apple trees at the bottom of our garden.

Not to be outdone, I decided I should cook something hot and spicy which might get things moving and spent a day and a half making a lamb dhansak, using a very involved Cyrus Todiwala recipe from his *Café Spice Namaste* cookbook. All to no avail. The lamb dhansak was eaten. Yvette was on the cranberry juice. The rest of us had another glass of wine.

The due date loomed. If nothing had happened by the next morning, we were going to have to go into the maternity ward anyway. That evening, Yvette was having some Braxton Hicks contractions. They were light and she didn't think they were anything significant, so we timed them but not very rigorously. Then, at about 11 p.m., as we were preparing to go to sleep ready for induction day, Yvette turned and said, 'I need you to time this contraction.' 'Fine,' I said wearily, 'just give me a moment.' Suddenly, in a piercing tone, she yelled at me: 'Just time my fucking contractions RIGHT NOW.' The immediacy, volume, pitch and post-watershed content of Yvette's vehement response told me this was no false alarm.

After all that waiting, things began moving at breakneck speed. By the time we'd grabbed the hospital bag and driven the two miles over to Pontefract General Infirmary, the baby was already arriving and there was definitely no time for the epidural that Yvette had been counting on for the past nine months. She was not happy. The swearing continued and became more animated. 'I'll deliver the baby,' the midwife yelled to me across the bed. 'You just try and keep Mum in the room.'

I hunkered down at the top of the bed, like a Castleford Tigers prop forward trying to steady the scrum, and the impressively calm midwife focused on the task at hand. In what felt (to me) like no time, our beautiful baby girl was born, checked, weighed and in her mother's arms. Exhausted, I slumped in an armchair and fell into one of those dark sleeps where hours pass in what seems like a minute. I woke up to find our new daughter sprawled asleep across my chest and Yvette sitting up in bed, looking out at the rising 7 a.m. sun and eating toast with tea. 'How are you?' I mumbled, dazed and shell-shocked. 'Fine,' she replied. 'But I could do with a bacon sandwich.'

If the waiting was interminable for our first child, it was no better for the second and third. By the time Yvette was pregnant again, she was a newly appointed minister in the Department of Health, the first-ever government minister to be pregnant in office, and with maternity services among the subjects in her brief. The baby was expected in August and, a month before, we were due to attend a family wedding in Norfolk. We had booked into an old hotel called Seamarge in a village called Overstrand, just south of Sheringham, where I spent my childhood holidays. It was the hotel Churchill would frequent to oversee preparations for a potential German invasion through Holland and over the North Sea to East Anglia.

But was it sensible to go to Norfolk, just a few weeks before the baby was due, if it meant being far away from the hospital where Yvette was due to give birth? Yvette asked that question casually during one of her regular meetings with the Department of Health's chief midwife. She wasn't quite expecting the formality of the response. Two days after the meeting, a paper arrived in Yvette's ministerial office. The chief midwife said she'd pondered the matter over the weekend and, yes, the trip was fine. But she'd enclosed a map of England sketching out the best car routes from Norfolk back to West Yorkshire so that we'd never be too far from a maternity unit should we suddenly need one during the drive!

Appreciated as it was, the chief midwife's map was not required. We arrived back to Castleford from Norfolk in early August and then waited a further three weeks. I cooked a wide range of spicy curries. Mexican chilli too. I must have planted at least ten fruit trees. Yvette painted a Winnie the Pooh mural on the wall of baby bedroom number two. My mother-in-law arrived but still nothing was happening. Sick of spending so much time at home, we decided to go into Leeds for an early evening drink. I ordered very spicy Bloody Marys for all of us – a single for me and Yvette, a double for June. And it did the trick. Six hours later I was shaken awake, the dawn light already creeping above the curtains. On this occasion, and again when our third child was born, we had the same early morning scramble, always with Yvette yelling and swearing at me to time her contractions as I desperately searched for the hospital bag.

As physically and emotionally exhausted as I was by the birth of our children, I knew it was nothing compared to what Yvette had to deal with. That first time round, we'd been arguing for ages over what to call our new baby, and we were especially divided on potential girl's names. But for all my advocacy of dads being involved in the birth of their kids, once I saw what Yvette had to do, I backed down immediately when it came to the new baby's name. 'It's your call,' I told Yvette. 'You choose.' I paused for a moment's second thought. 'As long as it's not Ophelia . . .'

CHOCOLATE MOUSSE

Serves 6

This is a dark chocolate mousse that you bake in the oven, perfect for pregnant mums who can't eat uncooked egg yolks. It's made by melting the chocolate into milk and double cream and then whisking in beaten sugar, egg yolks and vanilla to make a thick, steaming, molten chocolate sauce which you then pour into ramekins and cook for 40 minutes in the oven until wobbly and just set. I use a mix of dark and milk chocolate, but you can go all dark chocolate for greater intensity. Either way, they will be rich and chocolatey.

When cool, the individual mousses are great with something tart and sweet on the side. I usually make a raspberry coulis by slow-simmering the raspberries in a pan with a tablespoon of water and a tablespoon of caster sugar until it thickens. Leave it to cool before serving with a raspberry and a dollop of double cream on top.

Ingredients

- 400ml whole milk
- 250ml double cream
- 100g dark chocolate
- 100g milk chocolate
- 50g caster sugar
- 4 egg yolks
- 1 tsp vanilla
- Double cream, whipped and on the side
- 150g raspberries

Method

1. Put the milk and cream into a saucepan and bring to the boil. Add the chocolate and stir until it all melts – it will be easier if you chop or grate it. Set aside to cool a little.

2. Turn the oven on to 170°C/325°F/gas mark 3.

3. In a bowl, whisk the sugar, egg yolks and vanilla. Then add the chocolate mixture and whisk together.

4. Pour the mixture into six ramekins. Put the ramekins into an ovenproof dish and pour boiling water around them to halfway up the sides.

5. Carefully transfer to the oven and cook for 40 minutes. The mousse should be set, but wobbly. Remove from the oven and leave to cool. You can then cover and keep them in the fridge until needed.

MUSHROOM RISOTTO

Serves 4

Mushroom risotto is the first and last dish that Yvette ever cooked for me. It was a favourite of hers to cook when she was pregnant with our first child. Done properly, it's a rather fancy and time-consuming way to make cooked rice – which probably explains why, having retired from cooking when the baby arrived, she's only rarely made it ever since.

My mum used to make something she called 'risotto' when I was a child. It was a way of using up leftovers and I never liked it much, just rice, boiled and then fried up in oil or butter with chopped onion and bits of bacon or leftover chicken and peas. Yvette's mum cooked a similar dish every Monday, but she just called it 'fried rice'.

It was only after Yvette and I visited my parents in Italy in my twenties that we experienced the real thing for the first time – a proper Italian risotto. One of their favourite restaurants served a mind-blowingly good Parmesan risotto where, in the final stage of the cooking – the *mantecatura* – the chef would set a huge, 2ft diameter, hollowed-out Parmesan cheese on a next-door table, dump a hot and cooked risotto from a pan into the cheese, add huge amounts of butter and then stir vigorously as the Parmesan melted in with the butter and rice until rich, thick and silky.

The quality of the stock is vital in a good risotto – chicken or vegetable works best. And as I learned with my parents from that north Italian chef, the more butter and cheese you add at the end, the better it will taste. I love to make a simple and delicious Parmesan risotto. To make a mushroom risotto, it's best to use both fresh mushrooms and dried porcini mushrooms, adding the water they have been soaked in to the stock. I also like to substitute asparagus for the mushrooms, chopping up the tender tips to mix in with the cheese and adding the woody stems to the stock to give it an extra asparagus flavour.

INGREDIENTS

- 1 onion, peeled and finely chopped
- 2 garlic cloves, peeled and finely chopped
- 1 litre stock – chicken or vegetable – add the extra mushroom water/asparagus stems if using
- 1 tbsp olive oil
- 600g Arborio rice
- 1 glass white wine
- 150g butter, cold
- 150g Parmesan cheese, grated
- Salt and pepper

For the mushroom risotto

- 150g mushrooms, chopped
- 30g dried porcini mushrooms

For the asparagus risotto

- 1 bunch fresh asparagus

METHOD

1. Heat the stock to a simmer.

2. Heat the oil and fry the onions for a couple of minutes. Add the rice and then the wine and enjoy the hiss. Stir the rice in the wine until it is nearly dry, about 3–4 minutes. Then stir continuously as you add the hot stock, a spoon at a time. This process should take about 18 minutes, by which time the rice should be cooked. Test to make sure.

3. Remove the cooked risotto from the heat and vigorously beat in the butter and cheese for 2–3 minutes. Add salt and pepper to taste.

4. If making mushroom risotto, put the dried mushrooms in 250ml of hot water for an hour and add the water to your stock. Then add the chopped mushrooms and soaked mushrooms after the onions before you add the rice and the wine, saving some mushrooms for a garnish at the end.

5. If making asparagus risotto, cut off the woody stems and add them to your stock as it comes to the boil. Blanch the tiny tips of the asparagus in hot water for 5 minutes, drain and set aside; chop the rest of the asparagus thinly and add after the onions and before the rice and the wine. Use the blanched tips as a garnish.

6

FEEDING THE KIDS

Apparently, I changed all the nappies for each of our three kids throughout the first month of their lives. Yvette called it the 'Ruth Kelly Rule', after the former Member of Parliament for Bolton, who told a pregnant Yvette in the voting lobby that new mums had quite enough on their plate already and changing all the nappies was the least a new dad could do. I say 'apparently' because when Yvette told me this story, years later, it was news to me. My memory of those early weeks is a total blur and I have no recollection of any such rule being announced. I just did as I was told on a daily basis.

Yvette says she always gave up enforcing the Ruth Kelly Rule after the first month, on the grounds that I slept so deeply that waking me up to do a change in the middle of the night took as much time and effort as getting up to do it herself. I have no memory of any of that either. Obviously. But with Yvette drained by lack of sleep and breastfeeding, all the cooking and food shopping fell to me from the moment our eldest daughter was born, and that lasted a good sight longer than the one-month nappy-changing rule.

And that's how, without either of us realising it at the time – well, certainly without *me* realising it – Yvette fast-forwarded her mum's culinary retirement by twenty years. From the day our first child was born, she stopped cooking. And to this day she's never started again. Barely even a pot noodle.

It helped that I was so glad to fill the void, just for the want of something interesting to do. It's heresy to admit it, I know, but I found the first weeks of fatherhood pretty boring. I made cups of tea, answered greetings cards, accepted bunches of flowers at the door and changed nappies of course. But there wasn't a whole lot more I could contribute. The one asset I brought to proceedings – cooking aside – was my ability to jiggle. When our tiny little daughter was feeling colicky, I'd lay her down on her front, scoop her up with my right hand and start to massage her stomach while her head and arms rested on my left arm. With a bit of extra bounce and sway, I could jiggle for hours. All that hip action would come in useful seventeen years later when I started my training for *Strictly Come Dancing* – not so much when I returned to the Treasury after a fortnight's paternity leave.

While I'm embarrassed to say that fatherhood didn't disrupt my working life much at all, it was an entirely different story for Yvette. It's hard enough being a Member of

Parliament and having a young baby, but back then there were no maternity arrangements for new mums – not even proxy votes, where someone could vote on their behalf rather than obliging their attendance in person. In the constituency, there were still residents in need of urgent help, and a busy office dealing with day-to-day problems. There were still schools to visit, council meetings to attend, and speeches to make. And none of that could be done by anyone else – the idea of 'maternity cover' for MPs was, until very recently, unheard of.

If things were difficult the first time round, the birth of our second child created a situation that had never happened before in British politics. Yvette was by then in her post at the Department of Health, and therefore the first government minister to take maternity leave. Her first challenge was to work out what her entitlement to leave should be. Yvette spoke to her boss, Health Secretary Alan Milburn, who said he didn't know and told her to speak to the department's top civil servant. He said he didn't know either and passed her on to the Cabinet Secretary, the chief mandarin for all of Whitehall. He explained that there were no rules, and no past precedent to follow, and that, strictly speaking – since Yvette was a Minister of the Crown – this was a decision for the Queen, not the civil service. No one thought it was a sensible idea for Yvette to consult Her Majesty directly, however, let alone ask Tony Blair to raise the matter for her.

The Cabinet Secretary instead suggested that Yvette do

what she thought was reasonable, a splendidly old-fashioned way of ducking the issue. Knowing that she was setting the precedent for future ministers, Yvette decided she should take six months' paid maternity leave like civil servants did. The problem seemed solved, but of course it wasn't that simple. As a government minister, letters and papers continually pass through your office and every day you make decisions for which, months and even years later, you will be held accountable to Parliament. There were no formal arrangements for maternity cover and no precedent for how Yvette should keep in touch so she could easily return afterwards. The Department of Health and other ministers were hugely supportive, but it was an experiment in muddling through.

When Yvette had our third child, this lack of formal arrangements became a real problem. Where the Health Department had been helpful, the Department for Communities and Local Government was much less so, making it hard to sort out a plan and more difficult to return. Thankfully there has been progress since and – almost exactly twenty years on from our son's birth – when Suella Braverman was due to become the first Cabinet minister to take maternity leave, the government changed the law to enable her to do so. But there are still no formal procedures for paternity leave for ministers or proper maternity cover for MPs.

When my dad was a young father there was no right to paternity leave and no expectation that he would take any time off. The fortnight I took after our kids were born was only just becoming a formal right in that era. For me or my dad, the idea that some young fathers nowadays can take what amounts to six months' leave would have seemed incredible, let alone the fact that many will be the primary carer or share the burden equally with their partner. When I was a young dad, what I was doing felt like the cutting edge. Looking back, however, I undoubtedly could and should have done much more. But at the time, being in charge of all the cooking and shopping felt like plenty, especially having to make sure the fridges and cupboards were stocked in two places at the right times, so that there was something for the kids to eat when we arrived back in Castleford on a Thursday or Friday and then again when arriving in London after the weekend.

Once I got used to it, the online shopping revolution was a lifesaver – and I learned quickly from my mistakes. You only need to have 6 kilograms of bananas turn up at your door once on a Monday morning to teach you to check that you're purchasing by quantity and not weight. Ditto getting the delivery address right. More than once I've stood on our front step on my mobile phone while an irate delivery driver complained that I wasn't answering the doorbell, only to discover that I was in Castleford and he in London.

Once properly equipped, I embarked on what have proven to be two wonderfully satisfying decades of cooking for the family, although again not without initial difficulties. As the children were weaned off their milk-based diet, and after the fun and messy months of mashed banana and heated jars of baby food, I set about trying to get them to eat my homecooked foods. That became a frustrating struggle. Shop-bought chicken nuggets and fish fingers went down a storm, but as soon as I tried to make homemade chicken goujons or fish bites, they just sat on the plate, uneaten. They loved sausages, but when I made onion gravy to go with them, they didn't want to know. I bought cookbooks specially designed to be child-friendly, but, in those early years, nothing remotely ambitious seemed to work. Even when Yvette became adept at hiding my milk-poached cod in rice and peas to get it past our eldest daughter, our young son, a picky eater from the outset like his grandad, just raised his game, meticulously hiding the uneaten fish underneath the uneaten rice and peas.

Thank goodness, then, for birthday cakes, the one department in those days where my products were guaranteed to please the kids and keep my confidence up. While Nigel Slater was our top cookbook chef back in our pre-children days, Nigella came into her own after the kids were born. Not the flirty Nigella filmed hosting her midweek London dinner parties, but Domestic Goddess Nigella, expert in fairy cakes and buttercream icing. This was my most surprising dad-discovery: I wanted to be a domestic goddess too.

Our oldest daughter's first birthday cake was, I'm sure, a simple sponge; since then, the birthday cakes have grown in number and ambition, and once the kids were old enough, they were each allowed to choose their own design. I've made princess cakes, football cakes, a hamburger cake, an iPad cake, a Moshi Monster cake, a Converse trainer cake, a bouncy castle cake, a rugby league pitch cake, a Coca-Cola can cake, a *Doctor Who* TARDIS cake, an Instagram cake. Some were comical disasters, but the majority succeeded.

My favourite – and theirs – is the pirate ship cake, which they've requested I make a few times over the years. Most important of all are the decorations: what our kids always seemed to love most of all was the simple joy of seeing the sweets they could buy in packs in the shops popping up in a different context on their birthday cakes. Liquorice Allsorts may not be everyone's favourites, but they provide a wide range of options, from lifebelts and port holes to ships' chimneys, although, of course, only a chocolate mini roll will do for the main funnel. Curly Wurlys make brilliant fencing or netting (to stop the pirates falling overboard) and wagon wheels and chocolate fingers are enormously versatile building materials. Yvette suggested recently that I try to make sails out of chocolate: I discovered that by melting some dark or white chocolate, carefully smoothing it out thinly on a piece of baking paper, gently corrugating the paper, clipping it in place with paper-clips and then leaving it to set in the fridge for twenty minutes, I could make a set of convincing sails, fit to power a ship round the Caribbean.

Over the years, especially after I'd inadvertently gathered something of a following on Twitter, I'd tend to share each new birthday cake creation on social media. Sometimes people would ask me why I didn't include pictures of the kids blowing out the candles or enjoying their first slice. I explained that, for all the struggles Yvette and I had with parenthood, and juggling the demands of politics and family life, one really important decision we took at the beginning of our political careers was to keep our kids out of the spotlight. We decided that with each child, after a new baby photo in the local paper, there would be no pictures, no appearances, and we wouldn't name them in public. It's never been an easy rule to stick to because not only are people understandably interested, but it goes against most natural parental instincts to show your kids off or refer to them by their names. But it's not a decision that we've ever regretted for a second.

The biggest difficulty came when there was a direct link between our roles as a parent and our ministerial responsibilities. How could we ask other people to make sometimes difficult choices for their families if we weren't willing to talk about making the same choices in our own lives? That came back to me during the Covid lockdown when the government had to decide what to do about schools. I remembered a simulation exercise that Yvette and I took part in around the Cabinet table when the government was trying to control the outbreak of bird flu in 2007. As the secretary of state for schools, I was told it was vital to keep the schools open, because if every nurse and doctor with kids had to look after them at home, the NHS wouldn't be able to cope with the staffing shortages. That was all well and good, said Yvette, but if children were at risk of getting seriously ill with bird flu spreading fast in local schools, it didn't matter what the government said, parents were going to keep their children safe at home, and that included our three kids, so we needed to plan for that reality, not some alternative world where parents would risk putting their children in danger. Yvette was absolutely right: the basic starting point for her comments was knowing what she would do as a parent, and not expecting – on any level – other parents to do different.

The same was true when the MMR crisis broke out, when Yvette was the public health minister. A pseudo scientist called Andrew Wakefield frightened many people by claiming there was a link between the measles, mumps and rubella (MMR) vaccine and autism. His claims were unfounded but, by scaring many parents who then chose not to let their children have the vaccine, many children subsequently died from a killer disease – measles – which we thought had been eradicated. Yvette and I talked and decided that she should tell people that our children had received the vaccine. As the minister responsible, she couldn't stand with the chief medical officer and tell parents it was safe for their children to have the MMR jab if we weren't willing to say that's what we'd done ourselves.

It was the right thing to do, but also very controversial because – at the same time – Tony Blair, as prime minister, was unwilling to answer the same question about whether his young son had received the jab. The prime minister's office was cross that Yvette *was* willing to, and I don't think they forgave her for that decision. But, as we've seen from the same debates over the Covid-19 vaccine, it's vital for the country's public health to counter these scare stories and conspiracy theories, and it's impossible to do that if you can't say whether you've followed the same advice you're giving to others.

Gordon and Sarah Brown had children soon after Yvette and me. They too decided to keep their children out of the public eye. Tragically for Gordon and Sarah, that choice was cruelly taken out of their hands after the tragic death of their first child Jennifer in 2001, and then again in 2006, when the news was leaked from a hospital in Edinburgh to the *Sun* newspaper that their third child had been born with cystic fibrosis, something they had decided should stay between them, their son and the medical experts. It was an outrageous breach, and one which upset them greatly.

When Gordon was prime minister, he and Sarah stuck determinedly to their view that their children were not public figures and should be kept out of the public eye – until the very end of his prime ministership, when the family finally left Downing Street. It had become clear that Lib Dem leader Nick Clegg had chosen to form a coalition with the Conservative Party and Gordon and Sarah decided that they would depart Downing Street on their own terms. With cameras all around and a helicopter above, they walked together with their two sons down Downing Street for the first and last time. Their life there was ending, as was Gordon's career in frontline politics. After protecting the privacy of their sons for all those years, they decided their boys should be able to remember that day and have pictures of them all leaving the place where they had lived as a family and shared experiences which had so powerfully shaped their lives.

It's so easy for the children of politicians simply to become part of the backdrop for photo opportunities, and it's what the modern media have come to expect. But Gordon and Sarah never allowed that to happen, and – for all the other strains and stresses that our careers have put our children through – Yvette and I have never regretted taking the same approach. Our oldest daughter explained it to us one day: 'When I walk across the playground,' she said, 'I want people to see me for who I am, not as your daughter, the child of Cabinet ministers. I want to be me first.' At least in that regard, I hope we've done the best we could for our kids.

STRAWBERRIES & CREAM BIRTHDAY CAKE

Serves 10

With birthday cakes, most children only really want to eat the icing and the decoration – it will be the adults who have to eat the sponge. So if you just go for something sweet and sickly and not something the adults will want, you'll end up with a lot of leftover cake.

My breakthrough in cake-making came when my friend, Brigit, told me of a fantastic sponge recipe she had found in which double cream is substituted for butter. If you make this simple sponge cake filled with double cream and strawberries, the cake itself is infused with the richness and deliciousness of double cream as much as the filling.

But even if you're making a rugby pitch or a pirate ship, this cake is sufficiently strong and robust to deal with multi-layered design on the outside while the inside still tastes great (if you are building a cake with multiple layers, it's definitely worth cooking the cake at the higher temperature in the recipe). I used this recipe for my ski jump cake on *Sport Relief Bake Off* and then to make a pirate ship on *Celebrity Best Home Cook*. It's a cake which adults can enjoy just as much as children.

I've found that buttercream is best for the outer covering of the cake, but I've never succeeded in changing the colour with food colouring. So when I want to decorate with coloured icing – whether that's making people, shapes or letters – I buy separate coloured fondant icing and roll it out.

But always, if you possibly can, give yourself enough time so that the cake can cool. Then, when you smear on the buttercream, put it back in the fridge to cool before adding some more and then smoothing it over with a flat knife. It's so much easier to decorate onto smooth, cooled buttercream.

INGREDIENTS

- Butter to grease tins
- 350g caster sugar
- 300ml double cream
- 4 eggs
- 1 tsp vanilla essence
- 350g self-raising flour

FOR THE TOPPING

- 300g strawberries, washed, de-headed and halved
- 300ml double cream, whipped

Method

1. Preheat the oven to 170°C/325°F/gas mark 3 (or 190°C/375°F/gas mark 5 if you want a firmer, crisper cake for pirate ship building). Grease two sandwich tins and line with baking paper.

2. Combine 300ml of the double cream and the caster sugar and whisk for 30 seconds until well creamed. Then add the eggs one at a time, beating for 20 seconds between each egg. Add the vanilla essence and then the flour and mix until just fully incorporated.

3. Put the cake mixture into the sandwich tins, put them side by side in the oven and bake for 35 minutes before check-ing – a knife should come out clean when poked through the centre. When cooked (they'll probably need another 5 minutes if you have gone for the lower oven temperature), leave in the tins for 5 minutes and then turn out carefully and leave to completely cool.

4. Beat the cream until it starts to stiffen (this is easier if the cream is at room temperature). Put half the whipped cream on the curved side of one cake and arrange half the strawberries, cut side up. Put the other cake on top, smear the remaining cream over the top and gently place the rest of the strawberries, cut side down, on the cream.

SAUSAGES & ONION GRAVY

Serves 4

My first-ever trip to the Lake District made a great impression on me – and not just because of the scenery. I was ten years old and my dad took my little brother and me to visit his old biology teacher. After a long drive from our house in Nottingham, we set off the next day to climb up to 'High Street' from Haweswater and see the Lakeland peaks in all their majesty. What I remember best, however, was not the climb and the views or even the packed lunch, but dinner that evening: my first proper Cumberland sausage. My pre-vegetarian brother and I both loved it, and the next day, we visited a butcher's shop in Kendal and bought some to take home from one of the huge coils stacked behind the counter. We all loved the peppery, herby flavour, which was like nothing we'd tasted before. These days you can get Cumberland sausages with onion gravy on every pub lunch menu, but forty years ago this dish was only common in the Lake District.

Our children loved sausages when they were little, but doggedly refused to eat my onion gravy. No matter, because it just meant I could have as much as I wanted – a rare luxury for the father of the house in my culinary lifetime. Some people swear by frying sausages, others prefer to grill, but I always think they taste better when they are cooked in the oven and don't spit out all their juice. I use stock for this recipe, but you could easily use water with half a stock cube or, even better, leftover gravy from the Sunday roast.

INGREDIENTS

- 6 good pork sausages (Cumberland if you can find them)
- 1 tbsp olive oil
- 3 onions, peeled, halved and sliced
- 1 tbsp plain flour
- 300ml stock – chicken or beef
- 1½ tbsp Worcestershire sauce
- Salt and pepper

METHOD

1. Preheat the oven to 190°C/375°F/gas mark 5. Put the sausages on an ovenproof dish and cook in the oven for 30 minutes.

2. Heat the olive oil in a saucepan and drop in the sliced onions. Turn down to a moderate heat and allow the onions

to brown and caramelise for 20 minutes. Then mix in the flour and cook for a minute before adding the stock. Bring to the boil, stirring to thicken, add the Worcestershire sauce, salt and pepper and then simmer for a further 10 minutes.

7

WEEKEND COOKING

Yvette and I were the first married couple in British history to be in the Cabinet together.

A nice fact to tell the grandchildren one day, fingers crossed, and hopefully by then we'll have forgotten how unbelievably tiring, hectic and stressful that period of our lives was, and how weird most people thought it was to have a married couple both doing that kind of job. I used to look back on the Sundays of my youth: the rituals, the patterns – roast lunch, football, the BBC serial and Mum's tea, a true day of rest – and wonder what we were doing to our kids by comparison, dragging them down to London every Sunday evening for another week of work and school, before going back home to Yorkshire on Thursday or Friday.

Almost by default, Saturday night dinner became the highlight of my week, not least because it was the one evening I could guarantee we'd all be together and just be able to relax, eat and watch TV as a family. I would go to the butcher's in the morning and always have dinner ready for 7 p.m., followed by a film chosen by the kids on a weekly rota. Then, much to the amusement and teasing of everyone else, with dinner eaten and a couple of glasses of wine inside, the exhaustion of the week would take over and I'd nod off. I can't tell you how many films I've seen the first half of. Did the Incredibles defeat Syndrome? Did the Ents decide to help the Hobbits? I assume so, but I was fast asleep by the time they got round to it.

Carting our three kids across the country twice every week was a drag for them, but we had no choice. Our home was in Castleford and Yvette needed to be there for her constituency work at the weekends – a weekly round of visits to schools and local businesses, meetings with the local council or NHS managers and then hours of surgeries with constituents trying to solve every kind of problem you can imagine. But she had to be in London for Parliament during the week. Once I joined her as an MP in the next-door seat of Normanton, that went for both of us. It was exhausting and relentless but became normal for our family.

Our Sunday train rides down to London became an important part of our family time. We read, talked, played games, watched videos, and got to know the train buffet menu off by heart. We spent so much time on the train that the first words our eldest daughter learned to read were the station names of Grantham – which sounded like Grandma – and Peterborough. The travelling was fine until it went wrong: a flat car battery when we arrived late at night at the railway car park, or problems on the line, always guaranteed to come when the trains were most crowded, and when one of us was having to take the kids on our own.

On those occasional solo journeys, usually when one of us was having to stay late in London for work, we discovered an unexpected gender bias in operation. If Yvette got on a crowded Friday train with the kids in tow, usually wrestling a pushchair and clutching a rucksack stuffed with nappies and snacks, the commuters sitting close by – mostly men – would smile sympathetically, but she never got asked if she needed a hand. With me it was the opposite. When I invariably found myself struggling while getting aboard, I'd always find one of the other men leaping up to get involved, whether it was stretching out their arms to jiggle the baby while I got things sorted or taking charge of getting the pushchair stowed. Whenever Yvette and I tried to rationalise that particular piece of gender politics, Yvette always had the failsafe, fall-back argument that I clearly just looked more desperately in need of help than she did.

Either way, it was always a very different story when we took the kids down on a Monday morning rather than on Sunday night. Then we got the full-on grumpy commuter treatment, and neither I nor Yvette was going to be offered any help at all. On a Friday, the men in suits would smile and laugh when our daughter's toy talking telephone rang. On a Monday, they'd look like they wanted to strangle me with the cord.

I did sometimes wonder whether I was one of those dads too, glad to chip in to the childcare duties at the weekend, taking the lead on all the cooking and shopping, but firmly wearing my work hat Monday to Friday. We had Yvette's mum, June, helping out as well as regular childcare, and when in London we lived just a five-minute car journey from Parliament. But it was Yvette who tended to come back in the evening to read stories before returning to the House of Commons for the ten o'clock votes. By comparison, I worked my normal, long hours just like everyone else at the Treasury, especially before big events like the Budget.

My main weekday childcare task in those early years was to take our eldest daughter to the nursery class every Monday morning. I loved those short walks, chatting with her about the day ahead. But it was not without its difficulties. Halfway through her first year, on a Monday morning in February, we set off to school, chatting away. I didn't notice that the walk to school was a little quieter than usual. When we arrived, the gate was shut tight. I assumed that we were late somehow and everyone was already inside. I shook the gate trying to make it open, with my daughter holding my hand and looking up at me patiently – until the caretaker came round the corner of the playground and said, 'Sorry, mate, it's half term.'

We walked home, with me feeling a little embarrassed. I rationalised it as the kind of mistake any new parent could make. The following Monday, we made the same journey, experienced the same quieter-than-they-should-be streets, and arrived at the same locked school gate. It was an inset day. This time, as we walked home, my beloved first-born looked up at me with a disappointed yet resigned look that I'll never forget and said, 'Can Mum take me next week?'

Thank goodness we had my mother-in-law, June, to rely on. She gave up her job as an A Level maths teacher soon after our eldest daughter was born and regularly travelled up once or twice a week after that to look after the kids any time work got too busy or we had a childcare emergency. June would chat with them, help with schoolwork, cook their dinner, whip up yet another batch of pancakes, and make sure someone was there when the hours were just too long for our other child carers to manage. I know at times I frustrated June, arriving home late, making too much noise, bashing around in the kitchen and waking up the kids and her in the process. She was never shy in telling me either. But I hugely appreciated what she did for us and I think she understood how hard Yvette and I were working, and why.

There was one time, though, even with all her patience, love and experience, when it got all too much. I arrived home to find her slumped in a chair, shell-shocked and thoroughly outmanoeuvred. I asked what had happened. She said: 'Well, your son was being naughty and hiding under the table, refusing to come out. I told him I'd have to send him to bed. I said, "Come out now or I'll clip you round the ear." 'And', June continued in a bewildered tone, 'your eight-year-old daughter said to me, "Grandma, it's not going to work. Don't you understand? You can't use twentieth-century techniques on twenty-first-century children."' June was gobsmacked. And so was I. But Yvette and I figured that whatever else we were doing to our kids with our dysfunctional, itinerant lifestyle, it wasn't affecting their ability to get the better of their elders.

I knew life wouldn't get any easier when Gordon Brown became prime minister in 2007 and Yvette and I were both appointed to the Cabinet. The responsibilities were great – me leading the new children's department and Yvette in charge of housing – the working hours were long and there were regular evening parliamentary votes. Despite the efforts of reformers to reduce evening sittings, change was happening only very slowly. Yvette somehow managed to do her red box papers during the day, but I would return home in the evening at eleven and then spend a couple of hours every night reading and signing papers before going off in the car again at 7.30 a.m. I often didn't see the children all week.

It was hard for both of us, doing demanding jobs, struggling to look after three children under eight, all of us travelling 400 miles every weekend by train, dealing with the media and being a married couple in the Cabinet. Hard, but harder for Yvette. After all, no one ever called me Mr Cooper or 'Yvette Cooper's husband' live on national TV. The focus groups showed people thought it was weird that we were both politicians – 'Do they only talk about politics at home?', 'Will they make their kids be politicians too?' – but somehow, ridiculously, that made them feel more negative towards Yvette than me. That was especially unfair because, while I sometimes zoned out of family life on very busy days, Yvette was always present for the kids, taking their phone calls during the day and rushing back home for bedtimes.

Gordon didn't help when he moved the weekly Cabinet meetings to an earlier 9 a.m. start —one of the least family-friendly changes ever. Yvette tried several times to organise a rebellion, but to no avail. June would arrive on Cabinet meeting days at 8 a.m. and we'd rush out of the house into a car and arrive at Downing Street with a minute or so to spare, always cutting it fine but never actually late. It's no wonder we look a bit stressed and dishevelled in every photograph of us walking up Downing Street together.

Weekends were no better. We weren't allowed to take the confidential papers in our ministerial red boxes home on the train, so every Saturday morning the doorbell would ring at 8 a.m. with a postal worker delivering them by secure mail instead. We'd have Saturday and Sunday morning to go through them – reading papers, signing letters, and taking decisions – so that all the work was done by Sunday lunchtime, when the postal van would arrive to collect the boxes and send them back down to Whitehall along with the rest of the overnight post. We'd wolf down Sunday roast lunch with the kids, then whisk them off to get the train.

That's why those Saturday evening dinners at home in Castleford were so special to me: the one precious bit of family time carved out of an otherwise non-stop life of work and stress. I would shop each week at Farmer Copley's, a local farm shop in Pontefract, which sells its own beef — the best in Yorkshire – and we had it most Saturday nights, cooked in a variety of different ways depending on the cut.

I'd like to say no two Saturday dinners were the same, and I did experiment with different cuisines and dishes, including a wide range of Asian-influenced recipes, from Hong Kong-style stir-fry noodles to creamy Thai curries. Over time, however, we developed some go-to favourites; the kind of meals I knew everyone loved, even our son, and which I got better at cooking thanks to repetition and the search for perfection. Top of my list – as you'd expect from a butcher's grandson – was sirloin steak, coated on one side with a dry spicy Texan rub, served with oven-roasted potatoes, doused in olive oil, rosemary and garlic, and thick spicy Cajun beans, all followed by sticky toffee pudding or apple and blackberry crumble and custard for dessert. And I wondered why I always fell asleep halfway through the film that followed . . .

Happy as those Saturday nights were, I do look back on this period with a heavy heart. I tried to be a good dad when our kids were young, and I think they appreciated the shopping and the cooking. But I know I didn't do it well enough, and I know I wasn't there enough. It's a fact of life that the peak period of so many careers, the time when you have to work hard to make progress, is also the time your children are young and need you most. Doubly so if you live in two places and both parents have busy jobs.

I had experienced a temporary reprieve from the tread-mill for nine months a few years earlier when, in 2004, I was selected to be a candidate to stand for Parliament and try to be elected as a Labour MP at the election the following May. I had to leave my Treasury role as a result, but I didn't really make the most of the time it gave me. Yes, I dropped off and picked up our son from nursery school, but when I think about it, I should have been taking him on trips to galleries or museums, on boats and buses, to lunchtime clubs and children's playgrounds. I did a fair bit of that with him and the other kids at the weekends. But during the week, I always felt I needed to be 'working', one way or another, even when I was technically between jobs.

I do believe in life that it's important not to have regrets, to look forward, to be proud of what you've done. But if I could have my time again, I would choose to spend less time at work and more with all our kids during that magic time when they need a parent to take them out and enjoy the world. After 2015, when I lost my parliamentary seat and my life of regular nine-to-five employment ended, I did have lots more time at home with the kids, playing, cooking and chatting with them. But teenagers only want to spend so much time with their parents, no matter how much you want to spend with them and how many lost hours you've got to make up.

Back in my Treasury days, I persuaded myself that it was the quality of the time I spent with my kids that mattered and not the quantity. I suppose every working parent must believe that to an extent, but when I think back to the extra hour in the office I spent versus an extra hour at home, I wish I'd gone in late and left work early more often. And those pangs of guilt feel strongest when I think of how much my own parents sacrificed for me, my sister and brother. Before I was born, they were a globe-trotting young couple, living in America and Switzerland, enjoying new cultures, experiences and cuisines, and – after a 25-year gap – they were off again to Italy as soon as we'd all flown the nest. But during that period when we were growing up, all those desires and ambitions were put to one side, with not so much as a holiday abroad.

Looking back, their great luxury – not that they ever portrayed it as such – was paying for my brother, sister and me to attend the Nottingham High Schools. When restaurant meals were dismissed as an extravagance, that was where the savings were going. So when I feel bad about dragging our three kids around the country and regret those extra hours in the office that I could have spent at home, it doesn't help either of those feelings to reflect on how my own mum and dad always did the exact opposite.

However, I console myself with a broader truth. I look at my three kids now and I wouldn't wish for any aspect of them to be anything different. And I think – aside from my brother's vegetarianism – my mum and dad would have said the same about their three. So, however differently we approached the job of parenthood, and however differently I might do it if I had my time again, it all worked out in the only way that counts: the kids turned out OK and, in both households, extremely well fed.

TEXAN STEAK WITH CAJUN BEANS

Serves 4

I've tried cooking steaks entirely on the griddle or under a grill, but I think this griddle and oven combination works best. It's not how they do it in restaurants, but I think this is the most reliable way to cook steaks at home. The beans here are truly magical: rich because of their bacon base and chicken stock, and spicy because of the Cajun spice mix. And like Jack's beans in the fairy tale, something amazing happens to them overnight, so leave some in the fridge for wonderful beans on toast in the morning, and pop some in the freezer too for an emergency snack that keeps really well.

Ingredients

- 4 thick steaks – sirloin or rib-eye
- 6 potatoes, chopped into chunky cubes
- 8 garlic cloves, peeled and chopped
- A handful of fresh rosemary, chopped
- 4 tbsp olive oil

For the Texan dry rub

- 2 tbsp chilli powder
- 1 tbsp paprika
- 1 tbsp dried coriander
- 1 tbsp yellow mustard powder
- 2 tsp dried oregano
- 2 tsp ground cumin
- 2 tsp salt
- 2 tsp ground black pepper

For the Cajun spicy beans

- 1 tbsp olive oil
- 3 rashers of bacon, diced – I use unsmoked
- 3 garlic cloves, peeled and finely chopped
- 1 onion, peeled and finely chopped
- 1 tbsp finely chopped green jalapeño chillies (from a jar is best I think)

- 2 × 400ml can of black-eyed beans
- 400ml can of pinto beans
- 1 litre chicken stock – or 500ml stock and 500ml water
- Juice of 1 lime
- 1 tsp cayenne pepper
- 1 tsp ground cumin
- 1 tsp Cajun Spice Mix (see below)
- 1 bunch of fresh coriander, finely chopped

For the Cajun spice mix

- 2 tsp paprika
- 1 tsp ground cumin
- ¾ tsp cayenne pepper
- 1 tsp chilli powder
- 1 tsp garlic granules
- 1 tsp onion powder
- ½ tsp dried thyme
- ½ tsp dried oregano
- ½ tsp salt
- 1 tsp ground black pepper

Method

1. Mix the Texan dry rub together, sprinkle liberally over one side of the steaks and leave them to sit for at least 30

minutes. Douse the potatoes in the oil, garlic and rosemary and leave them to absorb the flavours.

2. Then, to make the Cajun spicy beans, first heat the oil in a heavy pan and fry the bacon for 3 minutes. Add the garlic, onion and jalapeño and fry for a further 3 minutes. Drain and rinse both types of beans and then add these to the pan. After 2 minutes, add the stock, lime juice and all the spices and bring to the boil. Simmer for at least an hour to thicken, checking the liquid to make sure the beans don't go dry. With 10 minutes to go, stir in half the coriander and sprinkle the rest on the top to serve.

3. Once the beans are simmering, turn the oven on to 190°C/375°F/gas mark 5 and heat a baking tray with a little more olive oil. When hot, tip in the potatoes, garlic and rosemary and cook for 50 minutes, turning once.

4. Then, with the potatoes in the oven, heat a ridged griddle pan for 10 minutes until it is very hot. Cook the steaks two at a time for 2 minutes on each side and then transfer to a baking tray. (Beware: The dry rub will smoke and make your eyes water.)

5. Cook the steaks in the oven for 4 minutes for medium-rare, 5 minutes for medium and 8 minutes for well done.

6. When cooked to your liking, rest the steaks on a plate for 15 minutes covered in tin foil. Reserve the juices and pour over the steaks when served, or you could put the juices back in the ridged pan and add a good pour of cream plus salt and pepper to make a sauce.

PANCAKES

Serves 4

Shrove Tuesday (Pancake Day) was the best day of the year in our house when I was a child. Just once a year, we'd cook pancakes, thin and silky, and then wolf them down, always with lemon and sugar. It still feels like a big event every time I make them. But for our kids – who will never understand the puritanical world I grew up in – it's Pancake Day all year round, and Yvette's mum, June, is the reason. She is an expert, and she uses the same thin batter recipe that my mum always used when I was young.

I love a traditional English pancake – they were the only type my mum ever made – but after years of living and travelling in America, I do have a soft spot for their more cakey, squidgy kind. Once you've had an International House of Pancakes (IHop) breakfast stack with lashings of maple syrup and streaky bacon on the side (yes, bacon and maple syrup do go great together), you never quite lose the craving for an American pancake. Little Chef have done a similar US-style pancake for years which our kids also love – good, but not quite up to IHop standards if you ask me. There are many fancy ways to make American-style pancakes, including with cottage cheese and buttermilk, but I have an easy and reliable recipe that I always use.

June advises that it's the pan that makes or breaks your pancake making. Pancake pans are cheap to buy, but don't last very long, especially if they are used for non-pancake frying. So she says we should keep a dedicated pancake pan and not be tempted to use it for anything else – wise advice all too often unwisely ignored.

Grandma June's Pancakes

INGREDIENTS

- 100g plain flour (or 6 heaped tbsp)
- 1 egg, beaten
- 250ml whole milk (or 1 mug)
- Butter (for frying)
- Toppings – lemon and sugar, maple syrup, Nutella, strawberries, ice cream (or all the above)

METHOD

1. Sieve the flour into a large bowl, make a well in the middle, and pour in the beaten egg. Slowly pour in the milk while whisking

until combined, then sieve the batter into a jug. (June says at this point it's a good idea to put your bowl and whisk in some hot water to ease cleaning later on.)

2. Put a knob of butter in a frying pan to melt and then pour a ladle-full of the pancake mix, just enough to coat the pan, and cook one pancake at a time on high heat. When you want to flip the pancake, remove the pan from the heat to allow it to cool slightly, which should help with the turning process and give it a jiggle first to make sure the pancake is moving freely before you flip. This amount of batter should make eight pancakes, but Grandma advises that the first one usually goes wrong.

American Pancakes

INGREDIENTS

- 2 eggs
- ½ tsp salt
- 2½ tsp baking powder
- I tsp caster sugar
- 30g melted butter
- 225g plain flour

Method

Put all the ingredients into a bowl or blender and mix to a smooth batter, then pour into a jug. These pancakes are better cooked two or three at a time in a hot, buttered pan, 1 minute per side. This recipe will make 12–14 smaller but thicker pancakes.

8

FOOD POLITICS

I think many interviewers fancy themselves as amateur psychiatrists, and one of the questions I was sometimes asked on the metaphorical media couch was how I felt when Ed Miliband and I were labelled 'sons' of Gordon Brown. I can understand the question because Gordon does exude a paternal authority; but the truth is my actual dad always had quite enough of a fatherly influence on my life, and an entirely welcome one too. I didn't need to go looking for anyone else to play the part.

There is one big thing Gordon has in common with my dad, however, aside from their shared intellect and their mutual love of football, classical music and family, and it is something I'm very glad that neither of them managed to pass on to me. Down the years, at least until my dad was forced to experiment by the lockdown, they have both been terrible creatures of habit when it comes to food, liking everything to be the same as normal – and as plain as possible – when choosing their ideal meals.

Indeed, during the thirteen years when I was working alongside him in the Labour Party and then at the Treasury, Gordon didn't need to choose his meals if I arrived at a restaurant first. I knew exactly what he'd want. French restaurant: a well-done steak with chips. Chinese: lemon chicken. Indian: lamb bhuna with a Peshwari naan. Italian: spaghetti bolognaise. And Japanese ... come on, can you imagine Gordon Brown eating raw fish?

I did once get the ordering badly wrong. One of my first duties with Gordon, before his wife-to-be Sarah had properly entered his life, was to help make him have a holiday for a few days, usually in the South of France or the Algarve. The only way to do that was for someone to go along with him so he still had someone to talk to about work. I could drive a car, play tennis and discuss economics and politics, so I was quickly judged to be an ideal holiday companion. On one occasion, we travelled down to the French coast for an evening meal and I quickly plumped for the *prix fixe* set menu for two, featuring entrecote steak frites. I didn't pay much attention to the starter course, and wasn't sure what '*huitres*' were, but I was sure they wouldn't detain us long before the main event.

Ten minutes later, the waiter plonked a huge metal contraption on our table decked with a dozen big, raw oysters, milky and fresh from the sea. Gordon looked at me in horror – he had never eaten an oyster in his life and wasn't about to start now. I managed to wolf down half of them and was starting to feel queasy, but the maître d' refused to take them away. Each time he glided by and saw the uneaten oysters, he just said something incomprehensible and disapproving, shrugged his shoulders and walked away. What became abundantly clear was that we weren't going to get our steaks until all the oysters were gone, so gradually it wasn't just the waiter but Gordon too, looking daggers at me, urging me to get on with it. I held my breath and slurped on.

Once we got into government in 1997, Gordon's simple tastes proved more of a challenge – not in the Treasury itself, where he would happily make do every day with the stodgy canteen lunches or his fridge-load of mince-based ready meals, but at the sheer volume of official lunches and dinners he'd have to attend, especially at foreign summits. Personally, I loved all these occasions: our counterparts across the world showcasing the very best dishes their countries had to offer; working lunches at 11 Downing Street welcoming foreign dignitaries; or slap-up meals at official functions in the City of London. For any of that to be part of my official job was a dream come true. But for Gordon, it was usually a nightmare of tiddly starters, haute cuisine main courses and fancy desserts.

Fortunately, one good thing about having an intense personality like Gordon's is that he could happily spend half an hour ignoring his Fugu sashimi or Matsutake mushrooms at the G7 dinner in Tokyo, while talking vigorously to his neighbour from Canada about the need for reform of the World Bank. When the offending dish was taken away untouched, it would just be written off as more evidence of how driven Gordon was by his work, not as some flagrant rejection of Japanese hospitality likely to cause a major diplomatic rift. Some people clearly got the message, however, and there was a notable increase in the number of business functions back home which started serving some simple combination of beef and potatoes if Gordon was the guest of honour.

Our first monthly lunch with the Bank of England governor, Eddie George, was such an occasion. People forget that – before we made the Bank independent – these lunches were major political and economic events, the informal meeting at which the chancellor and governor in theory decided together whether interest rates should go up, down, or stay the same. Perhaps because he knew these lunches would soon be a thing of the past, Eddie made the most of our first one. He preceded it by drinking a rather strong-looking martini, and then drank the lion's share of a bottle of claret from the Bank cellar to go with his roast beef. The pink-coated waiter then brought round a box of untipped cigarettes and another bottle of red wine to go with our coffees. Gordon's principal private secretary, Nick Macpherson, and I accepted both, sacrificing our health and sobriety for the good of Treasury–Bank relations, and Eddie visibly relaxed. Gordon was happy enough with the food, but clearly found everything else unacceptably decadent.

While fatherhood eventually forced Gordon to learn the kitchen basics, he had Sarah to thank before then for any catering he did at home. The Downing Street parties they threw together in those Treasury days, usually to celebrate a successful Budget or to thank all their closest staff at Christmas, were tremendous fun, with Gordon showing a side of himself – leading the singing and telling uproarious jokes – that the public never got to see.

Gordon knew by then that I wanted to stand as an MP myself, and his ambitions and expectations for me were always – if anything – one step ahead of my own, perhaps another trait he shared with my dad. But while he repeatedly told me his long-term goal was to install me as his chancellor when he became prime minister, the time was never quite right. In 2007, when he dangled it in front of me, I told him I thought it was too big a job to give someone as their first Cabinet post and – at the time – I was secretly relieved when at the last minute he changed his mind and I ended up taking charge of the newly created Department for Children, Schools and Families. It was a departure from the traditional Department for Education, rooted in the simple idea that if you are going to have a coherent strategy for how the government should support the upbringing of children in our society, it should not start only when they enter the school gates each day, and stop as soon as they leave.

Looking back, I am even more glad that was the post Gordon gave me, because – at forty years old – it forced me to come to terms with the fact that I had a stammer. As a teenager, I'd sometimes struggled to get my words out in class, especially when I had to read something out, and that had happened every now and again when I was at the Treasury. It only became really noticeable, however, when I first started doing regular TV and radio interviews after being selected to stand as an MP. After an appearance on BBC's *Any Questions*, my dad called me and rather unhelpfully said: 'You've got the same problem as me with your speech, but I don't know what it is.'

Once I got the Cabinet post, and was speaking regularly on TV or in Parliament, my occasional 'blocks' – unexpected pauses when I couldn't get my words out – became a serious issue, so much so that the Conservative MPs opposite began to fill the painful moments of silence with loud jeers. I didn't believe it at first when I was told I had an 'interiorised stammer', much like Colin Firth's George VI in *The King's Speech*. And when my excellent and caring speech therapist told me things wouldn't improve until I went public with it, I just laughed. No way. Cabinet ministers can't admit to a weakness. Politicians don't do 'vulnerable'.

Then it all came to a head. I had agreed to attend the launch of a special video for teachers made by Action for Stammering Children in which children with stammers, who had attended the Michael Palin Centre for Stammering Children, spoke openly and bravely about their stammer and urged teachers to give them the confidence and space to speak in their way.

Michael Palin and I both stood at the launch watching this incredible film, deeply moved. But afterwards, one of the children's dads confronted me. 'You've got a stammer,' he told me, 'and you don't say or do anything about it. My son is so brave and I think you're a coward.' I winced inside, made my excuses and left. Back at my departmental desk, I burst into tears – also not normal Cabinet minister behaviour. I wrote a personal letter to every child in the video to thank them, telling them that I had a stammer too and that they were a great inspiration to me.

It was the turning point for me, the beginning of a new phase in my life. That weekend I did an interview for a national newspaper in which I spoke openly about it for the first time. My seventy-year-old dad rang me to tell me he had just read the interview and realised, for the first time, that the thing he had struggled with all his life was a stammer too.

That decision to go public was liberating. The stammer didn't go away, but I knew how to manage it now and wasn't trying to cover it up. I became Vice-President of Action for Stammering Children and persuaded Colin Firth to join me. Together we have talked to many parents and children over the years about stammering and what we have both learned. I know now how much my stammer is part of who I am, that dealing with it has given me the confidence to do many difficult and fabulous things since. For that reason, I always tell the parents Colin and I meet that of all the things I inherited from my dad, I'd keep the stammer. Not necessarily the surname, I hastily add. But definitely the stammer.

In a way I never expected, coming to terms with my stammer also helped me explain the purpose of my Cabinet job.

If kids are struggling with an issue no one knows about – whether it's an undiagnosed condition like a stammer or having to look after a sick relative at home – it inevitably affects their learning and their behaviour in school, so, for the first time, my new department was trying to look at the lives of children in Britain in the round.

We could not have seen a better illustration of that theory than the debate prompted by footballer Marcus Rashford's campaigning in 2020 over the provision of free meals for hungry children during the school holidays. What Marcus exposed was the absurd contradiction of a government accepting responsibility for whether children in the middle of an economic crisis are getting enough to eat when they are at school, but not when those schools are closed.

Back in the late 1990s, Yvette – as the new public health minister – introduced a plan to give every primary school child a free piece of fruit every morning to promote healthy eating. Forty years on from Margaret Thatcher's abolition of free school milk, the story caught the imagination of the media, and in their follow-up reports, it was shocking to see so many children reporting that the fruit they received under Yvette's plan was not just the only fresh fruit they were eating that day, but the only fresh fruit they ate all week.

Almost a decade on, in my first week as children's secretary, I spent a day at a Banbury secondary school. The headteacher explained to me that the school paid for a number of children in each school year to have breakfast in school every day before lessons started. The rationale was simple: it wasn't just that children from the poorest backgrounds would not have had any breakfast, but they might well not have had anything substantial to eat since their school lunch the day before. If these kids came into school hungry at 9 a.m., they wouldn't be in a fit state to learn all morning, she explained. But if they got in early, spent an hour between 8 a.m. and 9 a.m. having some proper food and calmed down before the start of the school day, their ability to learn was transformed. We took the evidence from that breakfast club and showed it to other schools and local authorities around the country, so they could adopt their own schemes.

In 2007, another major issue we faced was over the standards of food in school, precisely because – as with Yvette's fresh fruit – the concern was that if children weren't getting some good healthy nutrition at school each day, they might not be getting any full stop. Shortly before I got the job, celebrity chef Jamie Oliver had fought a hugely successful TV campaign to improve the quality of school lunches, which led to new and demanding nutritional standards overseen by the School Food Trust, chaired by Prue Leith. School food was improving, but both Jamie and Prue were worried that many children were eating unhealthy packed lunches. And new evidence was emerging from a pioneering pilot study in Hull which showed that providing free and healthy school meals for all children in primary schools improved not just their health but their ability to concentrate and learn, too. The health secretary was Hull MP Alan Johnson, and he and I agreed to jointly fund some more pilots offering free school lunches for all pupils in a range of local authority areas across the country to test the idea further and make the case for a national scheme.

We decided to launch that plan at the Labour Party Conference in 2008 and, with TV cameras in tow, we drove from Manchester over to Bolton to have lunch at a primary school with a class of five-year olds. Alan was older than me, but thinner. He found it rather easier to sit down in the excruciatingly small and low school dining hall chairs than I did, and easier to get out of them too. As we tucked into our food and chatted to the youngsters, I became increasingly worried that the chair I was sitting in would buckle entirely. What an advert for healthy eating that would be.

Ironically, Alan and I had carefully checked the menu in advance to make sure it was manageable and that we wouldn't give the newspaper embarrassing pictures. Trying to eat on camera while talking to your fellow diners is notoriously fraught with difficulties, and you have to choose your foods wisely. Anything with gravy, sauce or rice risks ending up on your tie. Lasagne is OK, sausage rolls are fine, especially if they're from Greggs with individual paper bags to catch the crumbs, but spaghetti is a disaster and a pizza slice is impossible to get delicately into your mouth. Bacon and eggs are fine for breakfast if they're well done, and you can eat them with a knife and a fork. But trying to eat a bacon sandwich with stringy rind on camera is asking for trouble. What can I say? If only Ed Miliband had asked me in advance.

After the success of our free school meals initiative, I also championed the return of cooking lessons. Many secondary schools had recently invested in new kitchens to improve their school lunches and wanted to put their new facilities to best use. Teaching children to cook was a popular campaign, and a nostalgic one for many parents who remembered those 'home economics' classes from their own schooldays. After discussions with the School Food Trust, we came up with the idea of producing a cookbook aimed at secondary school children with simple recipes that they – and their parents – could learn to cook and practice at home.

Celebrity chef Phil Vickery agreed to write a foreword alongside mine and we both appeared on ITV's *This Morning* to launch the book and cook one of the recipes. We had just six minutes to chop, cook and eat a chicken stir-fry, while talking about kids learning to cook at the same time. Phil's speed and precision were brilliant. I just wished, as I saw the camera coming in for a close-up, that I had scrubbed my nails harder. That cookbook was sent to every Year 7 pupil in England for two years running. Michael Gove mocked it. But even now I regularly meet people, pupils back then or their parents, who remind me of that cookbook and tell me how it got them started cooking at home in their family.

While I was working on schools' and children's policy, the global financial crisis was taking hold. Although we did our best to support people through the crisis, with Gordon Brown leading the world in staving off a global depression, no one was surprised when Labour lost the 2010 general election. I held onto my parliamentary seat in Morley and Outwood, but only just, and it was clear that if David Cameron and the Conservatives ever won a majority in their own right, my seat would almost certainly fall.

We were exhausted that summer after thirteen years of Labour government. But politics never stops. Gordon Brown promptly resigned and the Labour Party plunged straight into a leadership contest. David Miliband, the favourite, was experienced and clearly talented, although, having worked closely with him, I worried he might prove too much of a policy-wonk. Yvette decided she didn't want to stand, feeling that our kids were still too young for her to take on the extra demands of the top job, so we agreed I should go for it instead. Maybe it was because I did less of the parenting than I should have done, or maybe because I was better at compartmentalising my time; either way, we thought it was more manageable for me. And I suppose, deep down, we knew my closeness to Gordon made my candidacy such a long shot that working out how I'd deal with the pressure of the job was a bit of a moot point.

Then, to everyone's surprise, Ed Miliband decided to stand against his older brother. It was painful to watch – two brothers and their supporters disparaging each other in public and questioning each other's personality. Ed's supporters stood outside the scores of hustings meetings we endured that summer with placards screaming 'Ed Speaks Human', an attack on his older brother, while David himself openly derided Ed's judgement at those hustings and criticised what he saw as his pandering to the left. Observing this fraternal struggle, I felt that a deeper family drama was being played out. This wasn't only a fight to lead the party; it was a struggle over the legacy of their late father, the left-wing academic Ralph Miliband. Standing in the audience at a London School of Economics tribute event for Ralph a few years before, I had seen this battle emerging. David spoke warmly about the man his father was, but distanced himself from his politics, almost dismissing them as part of a bygone age. Ed, on the other hand, spoke passionately about keeping alive the flame of his father's ideas.

In the 2010 contest, the politics were on Ed's side and he played them shrewdly. The party wanted a decisive break from the years of Tony Blair and Gordon Brown, and Ed was successfully able to paint David and me as their respective proxies; frustratingly for me, their fraternal struggle drowned out my critique of George Osborne's misguided austerity. But victory over his brother came at a cost, and not just to their personal relationship. In the years that followed, Ed, for all his talents, could not shrug off the image in voters' minds as the man who stabbed his own brother in the back, which they thought was disturbing and wrong; and Ed himself never chose to explain that he had done so to protect what he saw as his father's legacy. Perhaps that would just have added to the sense of soap opera, but at least people might have understood him better. I used to reassure myself that, despite coming third in the leadership contest myself, at least my family Christmases at home would never be as stressful as the Milibands'; and, as one MP said to me, it could have been worse: Yvette and I could have stood against each other. That would have been even more weird – although only just.

Meanwhile, as the leadership election continued, I sadly witnessed Michael Gove dismantling the strategy for children, schools and families that I'd put in place, and watched George Osborne take a hammer to the funding of our school-building programme and ditching our plan to provide free school meals for all pupils. I fought my best against those cuts, and warned of the effects they would have, but in opposition all you can do is complain. I had a painful illustration of that when David Cameron asked the maverick Labour MP Frank Field to review policies designed to tackle child poverty. Incredibly, Field singled out our breakfast clubs as a waste of money which merely allowed middle-class families to get cheap childcare in the mornings. It was a shameful thing to say, and had no basis in evidence, but my complaints fell on deaf ears.

Those years of opposition were tough, and there were continual murmurings against Ed Miliband's leadership. Yvette and I worked hard in our respective shadow Home Office and shadow Treasury briefs and landed some decent blows on our opposite numbers. In January 2012, we invited our shadow ministers round to our house with their partners for a spot of team bonding and morale boosting for another tough year ahead. I cooked the inevitable lasagne, just as my mum would have done forty years before to serve to my dad's PhD students, and our children toured the room with bowls of peanuts and crisps. It was a great evening, but we'd forgotten the cardinal rule: if MPs meet for dinner outside of Westminster, then they must be plotting. Sure enough, three days later a double-page spread appeared in the *Mail on Sunday* with the headline 'Ed and Yvette's Lasagne Plot'. We were accused of planning to unseat Ed Miliband, with the guilty shadow ministers in attendance named and shamed for their part in the incipient putsch. Of course, the fact that nothing happened afterwards wasn't taken as proof that nothing was ever *going* to happen, just that we'd been thwarted in the act.

While the Tory–Liberal coalition became less and less popular, at no point in that parliament did I ever think we could win a majority. As shadow chancellor, I spent the 2015 election campaign out on the road selling our economic message around the country, supporting our local candidates, and cooking lasagnes for our activists. But it was all to no avail, and of course – having spent more time campaigning round the country than trying to save my own seat – I found myself part of the wreckage on election night.

The next morning felt like a wake, for the party and for me personally, but the one thing I was sure about was that another five years of opposition did not feel like an appealing prospect. And, looking back now at the wild turbulent political years that followed, I'm not sure I was so wrong.

MUM'S LASAGNE

Serves 5

The *Mail's* 'Ed and Yvette's Lasagne Plot' headline gave my mum's lasagne a new political fame and notoriety. 'The Ed Balls Lasagne', cooked by the shadow chancellor himself, started to be in demand as an auction item for party and charity fundraisers, often raising thousands of pounds at a time, especially if I also agreed to act as the waiter – something I did once for Action for Stammering Children.

So, here's the recipe. It is based on how I remember my mum cooking her lasagne and so is heavily influenced by her Italian-American experiences on the US West Coast. Oregano is the magic ingredient and, unusually for a herb, it is better dried than fresh in this dish. I use Cheddar cheese, but you can mix it with Parmesan if you want. It also keeps well, in the fridge or frozen. If you want to eat some more the next day, you can reheat it in the oven or the microwave, but I think there is always a danger it will turn out dry. Much better to slop a couple of tablespoons of olive oil in a pan and fry the lasagne until it is hot and crisping up nicely. Divine.

INGREDIENTS

- 2 tbsps olive oil
- 1 onion, peeled and finely chopped
- 3 garlic cloves, peeled and finely chopped
- 1½ medium carrots, peeled and finely chopped
- 450g beef mince
- 400g tin of peeled plum tomatoes
- 500ml stock – I use liquid chicken stock as I've found beef to be too strong
- 400ml water (use it to rinse out the tomato tin to get any dregs)
- ½ tube tomato purée
- 1 tbsp dried oregano
- Salt and pepper
- 2 tbsp plain flour
- 2 tbsp butter
- 600ml whole milk
- 200g strong cheese, grated – Cheddar, Parmesan or a mix of the two
- Lasagne sheets

METHOD

1. Heat the olive oil in a wok or big pan and add the chopped onion, garlic and carrot. After 5 minutes, add the beef mince and brown. Add the tinned plum tomatoes (I chop them up in the pan), stock and water. Then squeeze in the tomato purée, season with salt and pepper and a good tablespoon of dried oregano. Bring to the boil and simmer for 30 mins until thickened.

2. For the white sauce, melt the butter, add the flour and whisk for a minute. Pour in the milk slowly, whisking as you go. Bring to the boil to thicken, whisking regularly. Allow to cool for 5 minutes and then add the grated cheese and whisk in thoroughly before seasoning.

3. In a large glass dish/roasting tin with sides, put a little over half of the meat sauce in the pan, cover with lasagne sheets, then spread over half of the cheese sauce. Layer over the rest of the meat sauce, cover with lasagne sheets and top it all with the rest of the cheese sauce.

4. Bake at 180°C/350°F/gas mark 4 for 40 mins.

STIR-FRY CHICKEN

Serves 4

This chicken stir-fry recipe is our kids' favourite go-to dish for a quick, tasty meal, and the first one they have experimented with for themselves. It's based on the original, simple recipe in our cookbook for secondary school pupils, *Real Meals*, but with a bit of extra spice and complexity. My standard version uses French green beans, broccoli and pak choi, but the kids are always inventing new varieties, including a vegetarian version without the chicken, and a fishy version using prawns instead. The lemongrass and ginger are optional and you can vary the amount of chilli, soy and fish sauce, or ditch them entirely and use a ready-made black bean sauce or oyster sauce. I like medium noodles, but thick noodles also work really well. Once you start, the variations are endless.

Ingredients

- 2 chicken breasts
- 2 tbsp fish sauce (for marinade)
- 1 lime
- 1 red or green bird's eye chilli, finely chopped
- 2 garlic cloves, peeled and finely chopped
- 1 stalk lemongrass, outer layer discarded and finely chopped
- 2cm piece of ginger, peeled and grated
- 200g French green beans
- 1 pre-prepared pack of stir-fry vegetables or a head of broccoli or 2 pak choi, big leaves chopped and smaller sliced
- 2 tbsp soy sauce
- 2 tbsp fish sauce
- 2 packs of wok-ready medium (or thick) noodles
- Bunch of fresh coriander, finely chopped

METHOD

1. Chop the chicken into bite-sized pieces and marinade for half an hour with the fish sauce and the juice of half a lime.

2. Heat the oil in the wok, then add the chilli, garlic, lemongrass and ginger and fry for 2 minutes. Add the chicken and green beans and stir-fry for 5 minutes. Add the stir-fry vegetables/broccoli/pak choi and cook for 2 more minutes. Add the soy sauce, fish sauce, the juice from the other half of the lime and noodles and stir-fry for 3 more minutes. Stir in some fresh coriander, turn into a bowl and garnish with a sprinkle more of coriander.

9

HOLIDAY FARE

When I lost my seat in Parliament in May 2015, we had already booked a special post-election US summer road trip: a holiday in California, with a week in a 32-foot-long camper van – an 'RV', as the Americans call them – travelling between Los Angeles and San Francisco. Out of Parliament and out of work, I couldn't wait to hit the road.

Holidays played a vital role for our family when Yvette and I were both in politics. They were an opportunity to get away from the Westminster whirlwind and say sorry to the kids for all those hectic months of late-night votes, endless phone calls and weekends spent campaigning. It was more of an escape if we left the UK – the more time zones away the better. And I was always happiest when the trip gave me the chance to do some proper outdoor cooking.

I realise now, looking back, that holidays for me have always been based around journeys – it's what I inherited from my parents and have passed on to our kids. Of course, when our children were very young, arduous and itinerant holidays were initially too difficult. Instead, once my parents moved back to the UK in 2001 and settled on the north Norfolk coast, Yvette and I set about reliving our own childhood holidays. For me that meant returning to Sheringham: sandwiches on the beach, pitch and putt when it was cold and drizzling, regular trips to see the lifeboat, and fish and chips on the seafront in the evening sun – the only place on the east coast of England where, looking down the Wash, you can watch the sun set on the sea. Yvette's childhood holidays were usually spent on the west Cumbrian coast, and every year we have travelled over to the Lake District to stay with her parents on a lovely small caravan site near Windermere, climbing up the fells and working up an appetite for Lakeland sticky toffee pudding.

As the children got a little older, we got our holidays back on the road, starting with car trips to Disneyland in Paris and the joys of the school holiday queues. I've spent more time queuing for the slow-moving Dumbo ride than I would ever choose and, unlike in America, the food was as dismal as it was overpriced. The hotel breakfasts each morning were an astonishingly brutal free-for-all of overexcited kids and parents desperate to make sure their offspring were stuffed with carbs before heading into the park. But with repetition comes experience. We learned that the key to a good Disneyland eating experience was to book a table at Cafe Mickey, just outside the main park. The food was still pricey, but worth it, especially because during the meal, Mickey, Minnie, Goofy and Pluto would come round the tables. That look of wonder on a four-year-old's face as they are hugged by their Disney heroes for the first time is magical.

We realised over the years that France wasn't very child-friendly when it came to eating out. We had one particularly bad experience in a Parisian brasserie where the promised *Menu Enfant* turned out not to be pasta or chicken nuggets but small portions of foie gras and snails. After that, on future trips, we opted for self-catering, staying on lots of caravan sites in different parts of France. As our political profiles grew, however, France was just too close to the goldfish bowl we lived in back home. On one occasion, with the children dawdling in a Calais children's playground, I shouted gruffly that they needed to hurry up or they'd be making their own way home. 'Watch it,' the man standing next to me said, 'that wouldn't look good in the *Mail*.' Trying to relax and get away from it all was hard enough without our fellow holiday-makers acting as freelance reporters!

Even worse was our experience with cruising. A few years earlier, just after the birth of our first child in 1999, my mum and dad had been enticed by Uncle Frank and Auntie Doreen into the world of cruising and we agreed to join them on a one-week Mediterranean trip with Costa Cruises, long before infamy and tragedy struck the Italian operator with the grounding of *Concordia* in 2012. The food was stupendous and just about everyone else on the cruise was Italian – almost all of them on their honeymoon. This, it turned out, was the tradition in southern Italy. After the wedding party, all the guests would come down to the dockside, the bride and groom would board the ship, and then, from the top deck, the bride would throw her bouquet down to the waiting bridesmaids below. It was an extraordinary spectacle, and made for an unforgettable journey, with the boat rocking at night even when the sea was completely calm. Our tiny daughter, then only eight weeks old, was captured on the honeymoon video of countless newly married Italian couples, usually being eagerly cradled by the bride.

When my parents persuaded us to go on our second – and last – cruise, eight years later in 2007 and this time with three children, it was a disaster, and not only because I was laid out for four days with a cruise ship bug. The food was bland and boring, and our fellow passengers weren't Italian honeymooners but fellow Brits. Yvette and I were by then both Cabinet ministers, and after a day of having our every move watched, commented on and occasionally photographed, we spent the rest of the time in hats and dark glasses. For the kids, though, it was a dream come true, with the all-inclusive package meaning all-they-could-eat burgers, hot dogs and waffles all day long. Our six-year-old son couldn't believe it. He was in heaven.

Cruises weren't for me and Yvette, so we turned to train travel. I'd always wished I'd gone interrailing when I was a student, despite Yvette's rather bleak tales of uncomfortable overnight journeys, dodgy food and running out of money.

So, using a family interrailing pass, in the summer of 2014 we set off by train from St Pancras and travelled all the way through France, Germany and Italy to the Aegean. It was a memorable journey, but Salzburg in Austria was the highlight.

The people of Salzburg rightly celebrate their city as the birthplace of Wolfgang Amadeus Mozart. Tourists flock from all around the world to see where the young genius lived and wrote his great piano concertos, symphonies and operas. If they're lucky, these visitors will dress up in their finest clothes, eat in one of Salzburg's Michelin-starred restaurants, and then see Mozart's *Magic Flute* or *Barber of Seville* performed in the ornate stone amphitheatre in the centre of the town.

However, Salzburg has an even greater claim to fame for families like mine – an even more vital place in our cultural history. Its fountains, amphitheatre, gardens, lake and nunnery evoke for us great songs of sadness, laughter, love and discovery, but not those written by Mozart. Because for me, Yvette and our children, Salzburg will forever be the location where *The Sound of Music* was filmed, making it the greatest holiday destination we ever visited.

I should explain from the outset that, if there is one thing that unites our family more than the enjoyment of food and the embarrassment at Dad's latest TV ventures, it is the love of musical theatre. For myself, I trace that back to my childhood, when my mum would sing along to *Jesus Christ Superstar*, *Godspell* and *Joseph and the Amazing Technicolor*

Dreamcoat. But I'd lost touch with modern musicals until my kids started performing in their own school versions, and we developed a shared love of West End favourites like *Les Misérables*, *Matilda*, *Rent* and *Wicked*.

Our all-time favourite, though, remains *The Sound of Music*, which we can sing off by heart, and in harmony, and which always makes me cry at exactly the same point – when Captain von Trapp hears his children filling their house with music for the first time since his wife died, instantly regrets his harshness towards them and their new governess, Maria, and ends up joining them in song. Love has returned to the house. It gets me every time.

Searching the internet, Yvette made an important – perhaps life-changing – discovery. A British tour company based in Salzburg was offering a 'Sound of Music Musical Bicycle Tour'. She booked ten spots for us and the Smiths, the family we go away with every August. On the train to the city, Yvette declared that, if we were going to go for the *Sound of Music* experience, we'd better look the part, and brought out curtain material she'd ferried from London for us to turn into impromptu neckerchiefs, headscarves and lederhosen, just like the von Trapp children had done in the film. The train was crowded but everyone looked German or Austrian, and seemed happy enough to see these eccentric Brits with their sewing kits getting into the Bavarian look. Until, that is, a fellow passenger on the next table leaned over and said, in a deep Brummie accent, 'We're sorry you lost the general election. Hope you get back soon.' I thanked him very much and resumed sewing buttons on my curtain-fabric lederhosen, feeling rather foolish.

Our embarrassment was quickly forgotten, however, when the tour commenced the next day. Each of us chose a bike and pulled on our costumes. Our guide had a boombox on which she played the appropriate song at every key spot in the town. We tripped through the Mirabell gardens, danced around the fountains in the main square, exercised in front of the big house by the lake, shook the gates of the locked nunnery and bounded through an alpine field, where the hills were indeed alive with the sound of music.

Interrailing was fun, but the opportunities for me to relive my Boy Scout days with a spot of outdoor cooking were limited. That's why my favourite family holiday is the American campervan road trip – driving an RV through the US national parks from Utah to the Grand Canyon and up the West Coast. It's just like camping, but, unlike a normal tent, the RV has bunk-beds for the kids and a double bed for the adults – Yvette's kind of camping holiday.

I've driven these huge RVs up steep mountain roads and through Starbucks drive-ins, into supermarket carparks and up and down the famous urban hills of downtown San Francisco. I love America, and I particularly love the kind of good diner-style American food you can find on any road trip. I'm always horrified by the huge portions and excessive menu choice – or at least I always pretend to be. I love BBQ, but also the taste, spice and colours of the Mexican- and Spanish-influenced cooking of the southern America states, and I've come to love Cajun and south-western American recipes inspired by American TV chefs like Emeril Lagasse and Bobby Flay. On an RV holiday, there is nothing to beat a good, proper breakfast quesadilla as the sun glimpses through the pine trees high up in a rocky-mountain campsite. And every evening we BBQ and build campfires to scare off the bears.

Sadly, on that 2015 post-election trip, Yvette didn't actually make it to our RV. Before getting the vans, we had decided to spend a few days at Lake Powell, a 200-mile-long man-made lake in the Rocky Mountains stretching way north from just east of Las Vegas. Along the sides of this huge lake are hundreds of inlets, mountain ravines flooded with water when a massive dam was completed in 1966, creating an incredible winding shoreline with a total distance equivalent to the whole length of the American West Coast. Despite its size, the lake can only be accessed from two entry points, south and north, where RV-style houseboats are available for rent, along with a small motorboat for exploring up the ravines. We had to stock up all our provisions before we boarded the boat and then travel off for our days of quiet, watery seclusion.

We had booked that holiday before the general election and before I lost my seat, hoping our holiday would be a chance to escape with the kids, who had put up with a lot; but once Yvette became a candidate in the leadership election which followed Ed Miliband's departure, we knew we had a problem. She was torn between the family holiday we were all desperate for and her need to keep travelling the UK in the final weeks of her leadership campaign. She and Andy Burnham had agreed early in the campaign they would both cease campaigning for ten days in August so their respective families could have some time off, but by now Jeremy Corbyn was surging ahead. No sooner were we out on the lake than her campaign team were sending urgent messages wanting her back in Britain immediately, and the phone signal, miles from anywhere among the mountains on the Utah–Arizona border, was very bad. We were also eight hours behind the UK, which was usually a great asset on our August holidays; this time it meant Yvette continually felt a long way away from what was going on.

We decided that Yvette would have to fly home early that coming weekend. But until then, the only place we could reliably get any phone signal was right in the middle of the lake. So each morning, at 4 a.m. – noon in Britain – Yvette would wake me up, we'd climb on board the little motor-boat and chug out into the middle of the lake. I then sat for an hour reading my book with the sun rising behind me, while Yvette talked over the day's plans with her campaign team back in the UK. I've thought about those mornings a lot over the subsequent years when people ask me if I miss being in politics, and if I would ever want to go back. I'm not saying wild horses couldn't drag me, but it might take a pretty big RV.

BREAKFAST QUESADILLAS

Serves 4

There's nothing to beat the thrill of a quesadilla eaten outside in the garden, on a boat or in a mountain campsite. The base recipe here is for a breakfast quesadilla – scrambled egg and bacon and all the extras. But if you're in a hurry, or tired, you can just roll all the ingredients in a warm tortilla and, bang, you have a breakfast burrito. They're also great in the evening with prawns and mango – just add mango instead of tomatoes in the salsa and prawns in place of the bacon and egg. Or duck with plum sauce. Or goats' cheese and chopped basil. Whatever you fancy.

Breakfast quesadillas work best when the spicy richness of the main filling is offset by cool tomato salsa, guacamole and sour cream. If you're camping, you can make them in a frying pan, but at home I think the oven is much better, as you have more control. Whichever way you decide, just don't overfill them or you will end up with a big mess to clean up!

Ingredients

- 4 flour tortillas
- Melted butter to grease and baste
- 4 rashers of bacon
- 4 eggs, scrambled with 1 tbsp butter and 1 tbsp milk, whole or semi-skimmed
- 1 tbsp butter
- 1 tbsp red onion, peeled and finely chopped
- 3 tbsp Cheddar cheese, grated
- 2 tbsp fresh coriander, finely chopped
- Cayenne pepper, to sprinkle
- 250ml sour cream

For the tomato salsa

- 300g small cherry tomatoes, chopped
- ½ red onion, peeled and finely chopped
- 1 tbsp green jalapeños, finely chopped (from a jar works best)
- 1 tbsp honey
- 1 lime, quartered to squeeze juice
- ½ tsp cayenne pepper
- ½ tsp salt
- ½ tsp ground black pepper
- 4 tbsp fresh coriander, finely chopped

- 2 ripe avocados, mashed
- ½ red onion, peeled and finely chopped
- ½ tbsp green jalapeños, finely chopped (fresh or from a jar)
- Juice of half a lime
- 2 tbsp sour cream
- ¼ tsp cayenne pepper
- ¼ tsp salt
- ¼ tsp ground black pepper
- 2 tbsp finely chopped coriander

Method

1. Preheat the oven to 180°C/350°F/gas mark 4 and lightly butter a baking sheet.

2. First make the tomato salsa and the guacamole – just combine all the ingredients for each in a bowl, mix well and leave to sit and intermingle.

3. Fry the bacon until it starts to crisp and then chop up into pieces. Make the scrambled eggs – put some butter in a pan, whisking the eggs with a tablespoon of milk and salt and pepper, and empty out into the hot pan and stir until they start to thicken nicely. Set aside.

4. Lay a flour tortilla on a board. Brush with butter. Place a tablespoon of scrambled egg and a tablespoon of tomato salsa in the centre of the tortilla. Sprinkle on some bacon

and red onion with half a tablespoon of cheese and half a tablespoon of coriander. Fold over the tortilla to make a crescent shape, brush the top with butter and sprinkle on some cayenne. Don't overfill or the contents will spill everywhere.

5. Repeat four times and put the completed tray in the oven for 10 minutes.

6. Allow the tortillas to cool a little, then cut in half and serve the oozing triangles with tablespoons of guacamole and sour cream and another tablespoon of tomato salsa.

BBQ SAUCES

I love to BBQ standing outside, beer in hand, at one with nature, shooting the breeze. It's why I've always enjoyed the traditional American-style 'long and slow' BBQ where the fire is alongside the meat rather than directly underneath, and the meat cooks indirectly over many hours in the hot tangy smoke before being basted at the end in a special vinegary North Carolina pouring sauce (See page 84). But slow-cooked BBQ isn't always right, especially when the kids are hungry and you haven't got twelve hours to spare. Then you just have light the coals, heat up the grill, toss on the sausages and get basting. The following are the two sauces I use all the time, and especially on holiday, one for more leisurely BBQs, the other with speed in mind.

Pork Loin with Sweet & Sour BBQ sauce

This rich, spicy and tangy tomato-based BBQ sauce is great with pork tenderloin, but you can also use it for sausages. It works equally well if you finish it on a BBQ or inside on a griddle pan.

Ingredients

- 1 tbsp olive oil
- 2 garlic cloves, peeled and finely chopped
- ½ onion, peeled and finely chopped
- 400ml can peeled plum tomatoes
- 1 tbsp tomato purée
- 3 tbsp brown sugar
- 2 tbsp balsamic vinegar
- 1 tbsp Cajun spice mix (see Page 137)
- 2 pork tenderloins
- 500ml chicken stock
- 250ml water

1. Heat the olive oil in a saucepan, add the garlic and onions and cook for 5 minutes. Add the tomatoes and chop them up in the pan. Add the tomato puree, brown sugar, balsamic vinegar and Cajun spice. Bring to the boil and simmer for 15 minutes to thicken the BBQ sauce. Cool.

2. Preheat the oven to 180°C/350°F/gas mark 4.

3. Smear the pork tenderloins all over with half the BBQ sauce, reserving the rest. Put in a casserole dish and pour the chicken stock and water around. Cover and put in the oven for 1 hour.

4. Heat a griddle pan until hot, then take the pork loins out of the casserole dish and reduce the cooking liquid on the stove by half. Transfer the pork to the griddle pan and cook for 5 minutes, smearing liberally with the remaining BBQ sauce. Chop up the pork tenderloins and pour the reduced liquid over to serve.

Rapid BBQ sauce

When you have to BBQ in a hurry, the sauce has an extra role to fulfil: to add flavour but also to provide a protective coating around the sausages and burgers while they cook so that, rather than the skin burning, you get a tasty, dark and caramelised outer crust. When I'm doing this kind of rapid BBQ, there is no time to make a complex BBQ sauce. So if I've not got a bottle of shop-bought sauce in the fridge, I'll just throw this one together based on tomato ketchup plus some other key ingredients. Better than a burnt sausage any time.

INGREDIENTS

- ½ mug tomato ketchup
- 2 tbsp brown sauce
- 2 tbsp Dijon mustard
- 2 tbsp brown sugar

- 1 tbsp soy sauce
- 1 tsp liquid smoke (or a squirt of a branded smoky BBQ sauce – no worries if you don't have any though!)
- Salt and pepper

Method

Mix all the ingredients together in the mug with the tomato ketchup and smear over the sausages on the BBQ or grill. Cook for 15 minutes until cooked through. You can always pre-cook the sausages for 15 minutes in the oven first, too, which also works particularly well for chicken joints. Otherwise, just keep everything turning and all will be fine.

10

EMBARRASSING DAD SYNDROME

My life turned upside down on 7 May 2015. After twenty years in full-time politics – as chief economic adviser, Cabinet minister and shadow chancellor – I was turfed out of Parliament and found myself suddenly unemployed. Fighting a marginal Yorkshire constituency, I always knew this was a possibility, but until the day of the election itself, I didn't think it was likely. After all, David Cameron himself didn't expect to win a majority, let alone have my seat as the icing on his cake.

The next morning, I spoke to my thirteen-year-old son to discover he'd sat up all night with his grandpa to end up seeing me lose live on TV at 8.15 a.m. Only then did it begin to sink in quite what an earthquake this was going to be for our family. My kids were upset. My dad was dismayed. Yvette was a bit shell-shocked. And for me, it felt very final and abrupt, like that moment of helpless resignation when you've rushed to catch a train and see it pulling away without you.

I was disappointed, of course, but also relieved. At least I wouldn't have to put up with five more years of soul-destroying opposition, and that was even without knowing how wild and divisive those next five years of politics would be: three different prime ministers; two more elections; the surprising rise and inevitable fall of Jeremy Corbyn; the country torn apart by Brexit; and then the pandemic. For all my experience in politics, I didn't see any of that coming in 2015; I just thought, well, that's that – what next? And the answer, most immediately and unexpectedly, was becoming a full-time, stay-at-home dad.

While Yvette worked long hours that summer in the race to succeed Ed Miliband for the Labour leadership, powerless in the path of the Corbyn juggernaut, I was at home for our three teenage kids in a way that I hadn't been for the previous sixteen years, engaging them in daily chats about school, homework, friends and life in general. Much like coming to terms with my stammer, a huge weight had been lifted. No more deep stress knotting the back of my neck in a tangle of tension. No more waking up at 4 a.m. worrying about a morning interview. I decided to be proud of what I'd achieved and move on – a lighter, happier and hopefully more thoughtful me.

And, of course, I was there to cook, and took to the task as though I'd never seen food before. It was like running a café at home – 'Here's the menu, what do you fancy today?' – I was so happy to please that I often ended up making three different dinners every evening. For me it was fabulous – and for our teenage kids, at least it was a relief to have one of their parents out of the spotlight. After a brief media fascination with me not just being unemployed but having the temerity to go out to the shops in the middle of the working day not wearing a suit, even the paparazzi got bored and moved on. Part of what had become my regular life – journalists and cameramen lurking on the doorstep vying for a comment; photographers waiting to catch me off guard in the street or snapping me looking silly at public appearances – all became a thing of the past in a matter of days. No more embarrassing pictures in the papers; no more segments on *Have I Got News For You?* or *Mock the Week*; I was officially a former person of interest, and the kids were even ready to let me go to the school parents' evening, so long as I promised not to attract attention. At last, I was just an ordinary dad.

While I didn't realise it immediately, I count myself very lucky that my departure from politics – and the time I suddenly had on my hands – coincided with my teenage kids discovering the interests they were most passionate about pursuing in their own spare time. I was able to get involved alongside them just as enthusiastically and enjoy marvelling at what naturals they were. That was certainly true of watching them perform on stage in musicals – something I'd always dreamed of doing but never had the talent or the confidence to attempt. And, when watching our two older kids try sailing lessons after school, I was struck that the skill I'd always wanted to learn since reading the *Swallows and*

Amazons books as a child, and had even taken a few lessons and courses in over the years, was something that came so naturally to our kids. I started out thinking I could – literally – teach my son the ropes, but I've ended up watching in wonderment as he has – literally – sped past me.

And then there is the piano. Our children were having piano lessons and it dawned upon me that I had wanted to play the piano all my life so if our kids could learn from scratch, surely I could as well. I signed up with their piano teacher, Lola Perrin, when I was shadow chancellor and, eight years later, and with more time to practice, I'm now working on Grade 7 playing Bach, Handel, Parry and some modern jazz. Although, while I have always just managed to pass my piano exams, the kids always did better than me.

So I've been happily eclipsed by our children when it comes to music and sailing. Not quite yet with the cooking, although they still have plenty of time. However, when it comes to embarrassing the family, the kids are happy to concede I am the undefeated champion. Personally, I think this is somewhat unfair. I always maintain that it's not my behaviour that's changed; it's just the extent to which my kids find it embarrassing, which is much more in their control than in mine. And this is itself just part of the natural progression of parenthood. Kids go from total dependency when they are very young to the seven to nine age range, when they are less vulnerable but continually need to be kept entertained. As they get a little older, into the 'tweeny' phase, they like to have us around, but preferably not too intrusive or visible. And by the time they become teenagers, we parents are generally expected to have the same utility as cashpoints and vending machines in terms of providing instant money and food, with minimum complication or comment.

Those teenage years are a tough period of transition for any self-respecting dad. Activities, phrases, clothing and pretty much every aspect of your persona, which you've up to now thought were normal and inoffensive, suddenly become excruciatingly embarrassing to a thirteen-year-old. This change, in my experience, is heralded by the introduction of the phrase 'Can you not?' into family discourse.

In 2012, I ran the London Marathon for the first time for Whizz-Kidz and Action for Stammering Children. Preparing for it involved months of training through the winter, often in the bitter cold and rain, followed by carb-loading in the fortnight before the race, which, of course, I loved. Shorts just wouldn't keep me warm enough on a three-hour training run and every other runner I saw in the park was wearing Lycra jogging leggings – so I bought a pair too. My purchases were bland, dark and discreet, but I faced a firm 'Can you not?' every time I pulled them on and strode down the stairs to the front door. My surprising solution was to make myself even more conspicuous – but less identifiable – by wearing a fluorescent yellow running hat and gloves. By distracting attention from my face, I looked just like any other crazy runner out in the cold. It was only when I took off the hat and gloves that I tended to be recognised and – thanks to my leggings and less-than-peak condition – mocked. From then on, fluorescent clothes became *de rigeur.*

Another 'Can you not?' activity was live tweeting while watching Saturday night television. I was what economists would call an early mover where Twitter was concerned and, despite a minor misuse of the search function in the spring of 2011, which I was sure people would forget in a hurry, I thought I was pretty good at it. I certainly found it fun, watching *Eurovision* or *Britain's Got Talent,* to shoot the odd, opinionated endorsement or denunciation out into the ether. While I generally displayed rather ropey Eurovision judgement, regularly slamming the eventual winners for being unable to hold whatever terrible tune they were singing, I had more luck championing underdog contestants in successive series of *X Factor.* It was all harmless fun until one Saturday in 2012, when Dermot O'Leary read out one of my endorsement tweets live on the show, and Nicole Scherzinger reacted with a ringing endorsement of her own: 'Vote for Balls!' I was quite pleased, but as my kids' phones started to explode with messages from schoolfriends, their own smiles on the sofa turned to mortification – could I please go one week without embarrassing them in front of all their mates?

And then I agreed to go on *Strictly Come Dancing.*

I had barely danced before I was on *Strictly,* but the fact that I wasn't a total novice was largely down to Yvette. She did ballet lessons as a child, and was always trying to drag me to dance lessons. We once spent a painful three hours in a cruise ship ballroom, well over a decade before I did *Strictly*, trying to learn the cha-cha-cha. And in that strange summer of 2015 when I was suddenly unemployed, we spent another three hours attempting to master the tango. We had arrived at a house we were renting in Italy with Yvette's extended family and the caretakers told us they could arrange both a tango class and an Italian cooking lesson. With *Strictly* not a twinkle in my eye – or a sequin on my shirt – at that point, I was far more interested in the cooking lesson. As Yvette and I lumbered back and forth across the courtyard to the strains of a flamenco guitar, our kids rolled their eyes and looked away.

Given my lack of experience and these acute teenage sensitivities, 2016 might not have been the best time for me to sign up for Britain's biggest live television programme, not least one with a rich history of making its 'stars' go way out of their comfort zone for the public's amusement and entertainment. At the start, though, the person most embarrassed by my efforts on the show was definitely me. Standing listening to the introductory video before our first dance, I heard the announcer say, 'Dancing the waltz, Ed Balls and his partner Katya Jones', and I had one of those out-of-body moments, looking down at the scene and asking myself: 'What is happening? What on earth are you doing? You do realise ten million people are watching?' I learned that week that if I looked and felt embarrassed and uncomfortable, everyone else would feel the same. Whereas if I threw caution to the wind, got into character and just went for it – whether it was a banjo-playing cowboy or a green-faced Mask – people were more likely to have fun alongside me, and enjoy what they were watching. As with my stammer, I learned I just had to be open and be myself.

Our two older kids were able to come to the show a few times, carefully positioned a couple of seats away from Yvette so that they would never be seen when the cameras cut away to her shocked laughter at the end of my routines. I know they enjoyed it too, up to a point. After all, dancing dads are intrinsically embarrassing, so I was only living up to type. But my youngest daughter was hugely relieved when it was all over, and I was immediately banned from attending any more of her parents' evenings, lest the combination of a shiny-floored school hall and a loud PA system lead to a clamour from the other parents and teachers for a quick reprise of 'Gangnam Style'.

The best thing about *Strictly* was that it took away any nerves, inhibitions or embarrassment I might have felt about taking on other challenges. So, even when making serious documentaries about the rise of populism in America and across Europe, I didn't mind when the producers somehow thought it essential to my political analysis to dress in a Union Jack-style leotard to do Saturday-night wrestling in Alabama, take a Taser shot to the buttocks while training with the Louisiana police, or have the same area rather invasively massaged alongside a reality TV star in Milan.

And of course, performing in front of a live audience held fewer fears after *Strictly*, even when I joined Frank Skinner,

Harry Hill and the George Formby Society to perform 'When I'm Cleaning Windows' live in the Royal Albert Hall and on BBC1 to celebrate the Queen's ninety-second birthday. Goodness knows why the BBC asked me of all people to perform this particular role; and learning to play the banjo in a fortnight was very tough. But I've always enjoyed a challenge; my younger brother was a big Formby fan so I'd seen all his films many times; and, it goes without saying, it was an honour to play for the Queen.

At the end of the whole event, all the performers were due to go back on stage to hear Prince Charles make a short speech and lead three cheers for his mother, and Frank, Harry and I ended up standing with the royal party in the wings as we got ready to go out. In my old role as secretary of state for education, I had met Her Majesty and the Prince of Wales many times, but obviously not very often while clutching a banjo. Prince Charles turned to me, chuckled in bemusement, and said, 'What on earth are you up to now?' The Queen was smiling too, telling me how our Formby tribute had triggered vivid childhood memories for her, when we got our cue to move forward onto the big stage. Poor Frank hadn't noticed and got the shock of his life when Her Majesty turned and loudly shouted at him: 'Come on Frank!' I've never seen anyone move so fast.

But Prince Charles had asked me the right question: What *was* I doing? I guess after twenty years in politics, I wanted to do something totally different. And I was certainly doing that. Even so, when I was asked to climb to the summit of Kilimanjaro for Comic Relief in 2019, I had nerves for a different reason, wondering if I was physically up to it. I was going to be one of the oldest of the group, which also included Little Mix's Jade Thirlwall and Leigh-Anne Pinnock, *Love Island*'s Dani Dyer, *Strictly Come Dancing* head judge Shirley Ballas, NFL star Osi Umenyiora, broadcaster Anita Rani, *BBC Breakfast*'s Dan Walker and *Pointless* host Alexander Armstrong.

Three weeks before we were due to travel to Tanzania, I met up with Dani Dyer – not the '*EastEnders* guy', as my daughter called him, but as far as she was concerned, *the* Dani Dyer from *Love Island*. We went with the BBC cameras to a gym in central London with a sports science expert, Professor Greg White, and climbed onto exercise bikes with masks on our faces to try out breathing in the thin air we would experience at altitude. The level of oxygen dropped steadily and, while I thought I was fit, it was proving to be increasingly hard work. We stopped after ten minutes to take an oxygen reading and I was clearly struggling.

While Dani got the thumbs up from Professor Greg, he looked at my reading and immediately turned white. He told me my oxygen absorption had plummeted and, in normal life, if I had turned up at A&E with a reading like that, I would have been transferred straight into intensive care to prevent my imminent demise. Our doorbell rang the next morning at 7 a.m. – Professor Greg had driven over himself to deliver a special oxygen machine. He told me I needed to spend three hours wearing the mask every day for the next three weeks to acclimatise myself and get ready for the mountain. 'Otherwise', he said, 'I don't think you'll make it.' I didn't know if he meant 'make it to the top' or 'make it back to Britain', but either way, I did as I was told.

I did well for the first four days of the trek as we steadily climbed above 4,000 metres, already more than four times higher than anywhere in the UK. The nights were freezing cold and the days long and arduous. We were up at 6 a.m. and walked for eight to ten hours, fuelled by three hearty and very tasty meals a day cooked by two Tanzanian chefs kneeling in the mouth of a tent with just two gas burners to feed all the climbers, film crew, guides and porters. The air was thin and we all found we were hungry, tired and sometimes unexpectedly tearful. Early on it was Jade, Anita and particularly Dan who struggled with the altitude sickness. We were determined that all nine of us would make the summit together, but at one point it looked inevitable that Dan might have to turn back. He recovered, however, and we were all in decent shape as we prepared for the final push.

We set off for our climb to the summit at midnight, fuelled by cereal, porridge, bacon and eggs, but after five hours of steady plodding in the dark, and with the sun starting to rise, it was me who was starting to struggle. Whether it was the thin air or the fatigue, I was having real difficulty focusing my mind on what I was trying to do, and all I wanted to do was sit down. Our lovely doctor gave me a steroid, a cup of tea and some biscuits and said that if this didn't perk me up and give me that final boost, I'd have to turn back. In that moment of crisis, it wasn't the biscuits that did the trick, or even the encouragement of my fellow climbers – it was the dreadful fear of embarrassing my kids. And that wasn't just in my mind; my son had told me very clearly before I left: 'Look, Dad, be safe, and whatever you do, if Little Mix make it to the summit, make sure you do too.' It was a high bar to set, given that I was over fifty and overweight while Jade and Leigh-Anne were as strong and fit as Olympic-ready professional athletes. But that was his challenge to me and it drove me on.

After six days climbing, just three hours from the summit, and with Jade and Leigh-Anne still going strong, I simply couldn't give up – not when I was this close. So I dug deep and made it to the top, with Dan and Alexander both holding me up for the last few strides to the summit.

I made friends for life on that mountain, and I was delighted to welcome them all round for a Sunday roast, followed by the kind of rich treacle tart that would have done wonders for our energy levels in that final stretch. And whatever embarrassments I may have put them through in recent years, I know the kids weren't complaining too much when half of Little Mix were hanging out in their back garden. 'Can you not?' indeed.

TREACLE TART

Serves 8

A month after we conquered the summit of Kilimanjaro for Comic Relief, I cooked Sunday roast beef and Yorkshire puddings for my climbing mates. For afters, I made one of my favourite desserts using a Peter Gordon recipe that I've used time and again and adapted over the years. Dan Walker is a particular fan. It takes a bit of time, and while you could speed things up a little with a shop-bought sweet pastry case, the 'sable' sweet pastry is easy to make. I usually make it by hand, but you could easily blitz it in a mixer.

Ingredients

For the sweet pastry:

- 150g unsalted butter, cold and cubed
- 250g plain flour
- Grated zest of half a lemon
- 100g icing sugar
- 1 small egg, beaten
- 1 tbsp milk, whole or semi-skimmed
- 1 egg yolk, beaten (to seal the pastry case)

For the filling

- 4 eggs
- 1 lemon, juice and grated zest
- 550ml golden syrup
- 450ml double cream
- 3 croissants, crumbed in a blender
- 1 apple, peeled, cored and finely chopped

Method

1. Quickly and lightly rub the butter into the flour – only take 30 seconds and don't worry if the mix is still a bit lumpy. Add the lemon zest, icing sugar and the egg and lightly mix into a ball by hand. If it's too dry, add some milk. When it's shaped into a ball, wrap it in cling film and put it in the fridge for half an hour.

2. Turn the oven on to 180°C/350°F/gas mark 4. Butter a round 30cm tin – preferably with a removable bottom. This sweet, sticky pastry is very hard to roll – I find it's much easier just to put it in the tin and shape it into the base and sides. Cut a piece of greaseproof paper to more than cover the pastry case and then pour baking beans or dried beans over the paper to hold down the pastry while it cooks. Put in the oven and bake for 15 minutes. Take out, remove the beans and paper, brush with some beaten egg yolk and cook for another 10 minutes.

3. Turn down the oven to 170°C/325°F/gas mark 3.

4. In a large bowl, hand-whisk the eggs and lemon, add the syrup and cream, then whisk until fully blended and emulsified. Add the croissant crumbs and grated apple, mix well and pour into the pastry case.

5. Bake for 40 minutes and then check. The top should be set but still wobbly. You will probably need another 10 minutes. Take out and leave to cool.

SLOW-COOKED LAMB SHOULDER

Serves 6

I learned to make slow-cooked lamb shoulder in a cooking class on an Italian holiday. The caretaker's wife from the house we were renting arrived with a huge shoulder of lamb and proceeded to layer an astonishing quantity of salt all over it. She threw in a few cloves of garlic and a sprig of rosemary, poured over some cold water, and cooked the shoulder long and slow. It tasted so good.

You can prepare this dish and then leave it to cook all day. The lamb does a lot of the work for you, sitting on the vegetables, with its juices flowing down through them to make the gravy. I've used carrots and potato with the garlic and onion, but you could easily add celeriac or other root vegetables. Make sure you pour some of the fat off at the end while you rest the meat, then carve the lamb in the tin and serve it with something fresh and green.

INGREDIENTS

- 1 large lamb shoulder
- 4 garlic bulbs, roughly chopped
- 2 large sprigs of rosemary, roughly chopped
- 2 tbsp olive oil
- A few knobs of butter
- 2 large onions, peeled and sliced
- 3 carrots, sliced
- 4 potatoes, sliced
- Salt and pepper
- 500ml chicken stock

METHOD

1. Preheat the oven to 170°C/325°F/gas mark 3.

2. Rub the shoulder with salt, pierce all over with a sharp knife to form small holes and place a piece of garlic and a sprig of rosemary in each one.

3. Put a tablespoon of olive oil and a few knobs of butter in the bottom of an ovenproof dish. Lay a layer of sliced onions on the bottom, sprinkle some carrots on top and then overlay a layer of sliced potatoes, seasoning with salt and pepper. Repeat and then place the lamb shoulder on top and season with pepper.

4. Pour the chicken stock all around the lamb. Cover with tin foil before placing in the oven. Turn down the heat to 150°C/300°F/gas mark 2 and cook for at least 3½ hours. You can go for a lower heat and leave it much longer, but do check it doesn't go dry.

5. You can serve this from the dish or transfer to a serving plate – but don't forget to pour off some of the fat. The lamb should just fall apart with very little carving needed.

11

FOOTBALL FOOD

A football pie is the king of pies. Eaten at half-time, standing out in the cold, scraped straight out of the foil with a plastic spoon or devoured with big direct bites into the soft pastry and its wondrous hot filling – heaven. My football pie of choice is steak and kidney, but I'd always choose a Cornish pasty over chicken and mushroom, and I'd take both over the vegetarian option. I know the idea of 'meat and potato' may put some people off with its ambiguity, but I've always found them very tasty – even if you're not quite sure what you're eating.

I know my football pies. So when, on *Sport Relief Bake Off*, our 'blind challenge' was to make a football pie, I inwardly cheered. The filling was mince, my pastry rolled out nicely and when it came out of the oven, the pie looked lovely, brown and gleaming with a little pastry football on top. Then came the judging and – like a dodgy handball awarded by VAR – Mary Berry and Paul Hollywood ruled against me on the grounds that my pie had a 'soggy bottom'. My face held a fixed grin but inside I roared my outraged dissent.

Of course it had a soggy bottom. It's a football pie. How on earth are you supposed to eat it otherwise? You can't scrape hard pastry out of a foil casing with a plastic spoon, let alone your fingers. A good football pie is supposed to be crisp on top, and squidgy at the bottom. But there was no point in arguing with the refs. That was the end of the matter. Well, almost the end. The burning sense of injustice I felt that day has further fuelled my pie-eating habit. Every football match I go to, I queue up for a pie to check if it has a soft bottom, as every good football pie should. And they all do. Obviously.

Back then, the only club failing my soggy test was my own team, Norwich City. The great TV chef and football lover Delia Smith has owned the club now for well over twenty years, and, not surprisingly, our catering is second to none, thanks to Delia's rigorous standards. Indeed, for a time, her own catering company was supplying the snack bar behind the Upper Barclay where we had our season tickets. The range of pies was wide and exotic – from beef in red wine gravy to ham and stilton – and the pastry was immaculate: crispy top and bottom. They were lovely pies, if rather unlike *traditional* football pies with soggy bottoms. But time moves on. Delia continues to keep a very close eye on the catering, but the club has since signed a new sponsorship deal with Pukka Pies, a favourite of football fans up and down the land. Normal service has resumed in the Upper Barclay.

My family has been supporting Norwich City for longer

than I can remember. Even though my dad lost his own father very young, that legacy of support was firmly passed on to him when my grandfather would head over from his Saturday shift at the local gas company for his second job working the turnstiles at Carrow Road and let my dad and his brothers jump over for free. Dad made sure I got introduced to City nice and early too, buying me my first yellow and green kit when I was five and, the next year, taking me to my first match, against the mighty Leeds United in the FA Cup. I've followed Norwich all over the country since, sometimes in the top division, sometimes in the second, and one year in the third. And I've eaten my share of football food wherever I've been, joining queues long and short, for pies good and bad.

Charlton Athletic do a good pie, as do Sheffield Wednesday. But the fanciest food I've had in recent years at the away end was at the sparkling new Tottenham Hotspur stadium. It was a memorable evening, and not just because Norwich knocked Spurs out of the Cup. There were over 8,000 of us behind the goal and the state-of-the-art bars at the away end ran out of beer before half-time. Delia didn't have to encourage us to sing that night.

Our kids are all now Norwich fans, as are my brother's son and daughter too. But it took some effort, and we both found that bribery with food worked best – a Coke in the car, doughnuts on arrival and a hot dog at half-time. The turning point came at Hartlepool FC in August 2009. We were guests of the club, with local MP Ian Wright, and the kindly Hartlepool chairman noticed that my son, a notoriously fussy eater, wasn't liking the 'carvery' food on offer. 'Hang on a sec,' he declared, and slipped out to a stall behind the main stand, returning with a huge hot dog, as long as my son's arm. And we won.

Over the years, on Boxing Day or the weekend before Christmas, we've had great days out at the football. Sometimes the fans in the family would go to the game before returning home for lasagne and strawberry pavlova – my dad's usual post-match menu request. Other times our whole family gathered at Carrow Road to have a big family lunch in one of the club suites beforehand. My mum and Yvette didn't stay for the actual game, but they were very approving of the catering. I could only join the steward at the gate in rolling my eyes when he asked them for their tickets and they explained they were only there for the lunch, not for the match.

My football food experience ticked up a major notch when, after the 2015 election, Delia asked me to become a director of the club and chairman of the board. I said yes without a thought – my driving ambition as a child was to play for Norwich City and, while I don't think my five-year-old self knew what a chairman was, I'm sure he'd have been very surprised and pleased to find out that's what he would become. The home games became an even better day out. Sitting in the directors' dining room, it was my job to host the chairman and chief executive of the visiting clubs, and talk football, business and a fair bit of politics.

The visitors were always hugely appreciative of the

catering – Norwich City may not have won many league titles or cups, but after twenty years of ownership, Delia and her husband Michael rightly pride themselves not just that this is a community club with strong values and a great family atmosphere, but that it has the best catering anywhere in British football. The annual award for best directors' room food has been won by Delia's team more than once.

My son and younger daughter came to lots of games during the three years I was chairman, smartly dressed and always impeccably behaved. Which is more than could be said for my very own 'Embarrassing Dad'. My dad is a contrarian and loves to provoke an argument. All my life he has been keen to share his, often critical, views about Norwich City while sitting at home with my uncles and cousins. They always berated the owners, board, chairman, manager and players, and that didn't change despite my elevation. Indeed, so much of the abuse given out by my dad and our extended family ended up being directed towards me, that I was regularly forced to explain that I neither picked the team, dictated the corner routines, or personally took the penalties. However, all that was fine when it was done within the bounds of our house. When you're the chairman of the club, however, sitting in the director's room, and your dad decides to lean over the table and say, very loudly, to the chairman of the visiting club, 'Our manager's useless, he's always too late with substitutes, I just can't get our Chairman to listen', what can I say? And my kids thought they had it bad with me . . .

If home games were normally a good day out, depending on the result and my dad's comments, away games were always much harder. There's a camaraderie in travelling to different grounds when you're part of a few thousand fans at the away end, but when there are just a handful of you stuck in the main stand next to the home directors, the atmosphere could be hostile, even in the boardroom itself. Some Premier League clubs were friendly and relaxed, but others were snooty and unwelcoming, with some owners and directors even sitting in a wholly different room. There were clubs who took pride in their catering – Burton Albion in the Championship was particularly good – but others clearly couldn't care less. One Premier League club had a directors' room which resembled a sleazy nightclub with dimmed lights, loud music and trays of off-tasting sushi. Others were very disapproving of our kids wearing their Norwich City shirts, and some even insisted on them passing the same full formal dress code at the entrance as the adult guests. My seven-year-old nephew's trick was to wear his shirt and (elasticated) tie over his yellow and green kit and then pop to the bathroom to swap them round once we were in. Even at our bitter rivals Ipswich, the home directors thought that was brilliant commitment to the cause. At deeply traditional Arsenal, however, they were not at all impressed.

Win or lose, it was never fun being an away director after a game. It's frowned upon to start celebrating a win, so you must hide your smiles and suppress your fist pumps. And if you lose, it's much worse – you must keep smiling while all the home directors and their friends are in jubilant mood. Those days you just want to leave – and the sooner the better. Throughout the leagues, the directors' room also remains a very male-dominated environment. I remember back in the late 1990s going to a match at Villa Park as a guest of Brenda Price, who had taken over my friend and colleague Geoffrey Robinson's majority stake in Coventry City when he'd become a Treasury minister. When we arrived, we discovered that the Villa owner, Doug Ellis, had banned women from his lounge, even if they were a director of the visiting football club. Brenda was told she should stay outside and we of course stayed outside with her. Delia has many similar stories of the ridiculous and odious prejudice she has endured over the years.

It wasn't just football running to catch up back then. When Yvette became the Labour candidate for Pontefract and Castleford in 1997, we were guests of the Club directors for Castleford Tigers' rugby league match against Warrington Wolves. When they asked her onto the pitch before the game, Yvette thought it was to say a few words to the crowd; instead, they asked her to perform the ceremonial kick-off, not an invitation to relish when wearing high-heeled boots. After the match, we were invited to the directors' lounge for a cup of tea, but when we arrived, the club secretary was waiting for us at the door, looking rather red-faced. He explained that the Castleford directors had two rules: no women in the lounge after a game and no spouses. The directors, he explained, had spoken at half-time and agreed they could break one rule, but it was asking too much to break both. So I stood outside and waited for twenty minutes while Yvette said her thank yous to the assembled men inside.

Our society has changed so much since then (and Cas Tigers changed decades ago), but what's fascinating about football is that it's been the place down the years where you can simultaneously see barriers very visibly being challenged, yet also the fierce effort that opponents of change make to keep them up. When West Bromwich Albion came to Norfolk in the late 1970s, with pioneering black footballers Cyril Regis, Laurie Cunningham and Brendan Batson in their team, I can remember the open racism they faced from some of my fellow Norwich supporters. But in 1979, their visit coincided with the league debut of one of our own first black players, Justin Fashanu, a great striker who scored the goal of the season against Liverpool the following year and rapidly became every Norwich schoolboy's favourite player. But even while breaking down a lot of the racial prejudice ranged against him, Justin had to hide his sexuality until near the end of his career, and the abuse and rejection he suffered after finally coming out as gay contributed to the desperation he felt when he took his own life at the young age of thirty-seven.

Times do change and the unfamiliar can become accepted, normal, celebrated. When my Uncle Tom, my mum's brother, decided to come out in the late 1980s, he told me, his eighteen-year-old nephew, but could not tell my parents because he feared they wouldn't understand. Over time, however, his partner Glenn became a valued part of the extended family and were both together at the party to celebrate my parents' fortieth wedding anniversary in 2001. Tom died of cancer three years later, before the new civil partnerships legislation had passed into law. Today, if he were still alive, I know my whole family would be sitting with him and Glenn at Christmas, looking at the photo albums of the civil partnership or marriage ceremony they would have held and remembering a special day.

Society may have moved on, but sadly football hasn't. Even today, no Premier League player has yet followed the brave and pioneering example of rugby's Gareth Thomas and come out publicly while still at the top of their game. My football club, Norwich City, has worked tirelessly to combat homophobia and racism, but we see time and time again how rife those prejudices still are in modern football and the abuse players suffer online.

If there's one area where I believe football has shown a truly positive lead for society, however, it has been in accepting and embracing different nationalities, celebrating what they can bring to our clubs, and by extension our communities and country. Sure, there's nothing football fans love more than a local boy who's worked his way up through the youth teams, and at Norwich, we still list with pride the players from our club – like Justin Fashanu – who've gone on to represent England. But at the same time, we chant the names of players who were born in Argentina, Cuba and Scandinavia, and take them to our hearts precisely because they've travelled halfway around the world to wear our shirt and do their best to make us happy.

When it came to recruiting a new manager in 2017, the process was led by our sporting director, Stuart Webber, who scoured the world for the right person and the best fit for our club, and narrowed it down to two candidates, one English and one German. The rest of the board and I enthusiastically backed his preferred choice, the German Daniel Farke. While foreign-born players had been in the majority in the Norwich squad for a few years by then, Daniel became our first non-British manager. As a board, we didn't think that was an issue, but it certainly attracted comment in the local press and among fans – some negative, but much of it positive.

The first year was tough for Daniel, as the players adapted to his new playing style. But a stunning second campaign ended in Norwich winning the championship and promotion to the Premier League. Daniel became a huge fans' favourite, earning his own song – a version of Blur's hit, 'Parklife' – and his own special culinary recognition at the many food stalls around Carrow Road. Now, alongside the usual football pies, fish and chips and hot dogs, you can buy Currywurst, Berlin-style – a spicy, curry-flavoured sausage which has proved such a success it is now also regularly appearing on Delia's menu in the directors' dining room – a culinary homage to our German manager. At Norwich, that's when you know you've really made it.

CURRYWURST

Serves 27,359

The people of Norfolk buying Currywurst hot dogs to show their support for Norwich City's German manager is an acute reflection of modern global Britain. I'm no expert in German cooking, but I've had a few Currywursts in my time, in Berlin and more recently at Carrow Road (ground capacity 27,359). You ought to use a Bratwurst or other German sausage for this recipe, but I reckon any good sausage will do. It's simple but good and should be served in a white roll.

Ingredients

- 2 tbsp vegetable or groundnut oil
- 1 onion, peeled and finely chopped
- 1 tbsp curry powder
- 1 tbsp hot paprika – or use a mix of ordinary paprika and chilli powder
- 400g tin of chopped tomatoes
- 100g caster sugar
- 80ml red wine vinegar
- ½ tsp salt

Method

Heat the oil in a pan, add the onion and cook slowly until soft, about 10 minutes. Add the curry powder and hot paprika and cook for a further minute, then add the tomatoes, sugar, red wine vinegar and salt and bring to the boil, mixing well. Reduce the heat to low and simmer for 30 minutes to thicken and allow the flavours to intensify. Then smear over your cooked sausages of choice.

STRAWBERRY PAVLOVA

Serves 10

The food in the Norwich City director's dining room is excellent every week and all the recipes are Delia's own. I was there for pretty much every game when I was chairman and still pop in for lunch every now and then in my role as vice-president and club ambassador, an honour I share with fervent City fan, Sir Stephen Fry. They regularly serve beautiful fish, tasty casseroles and an excellent Thai curry before the game, and the half-time sausage rolls and cakes are legendary. They also do terrific desserts, including ginger puddings, lemon meringue pie and a particularly good pavlova. These days we are back sitting in the stand and only occasionally go in the directors' box, but I will often make pavlova to eat when we get back to my parents' house after the game. You have to plan ahead if you want to cook it yourself, as they're much better if they have time to cool and dry in the oven, but I think there is no better consolation after an unlucky home defeat than a big pavlova, oozing with fresh, whipped double cream and fresh fruit – preferably strawberries or raspberries.

Ingredients

- 8 egg whites
- 450g caster sugar
- 1 tsp vanilla essence
- 600ml double cream, whipped
- 1 tbsp icing sugar (optional)
- Strawberries, raspberries or any other soft fruit, washed, chopped and sprinkled with caster sugar

Method

1. Turn the oven on to 170°C/325°F/gas mark 3 and cut a piece of greaseproof paper big enough to cover a large baking tray.

2. Separate eight eggs and put the whites into a bowl (the yolks can be used for a Hollandaise sauce if you fancy Eggs Benedict). Using an electric mixer, beat the whites until you have stiff peaks – the egg white should stand up straight when you fluff them up.

3. Now add the sugar slowly into the whites, beating thoroughly with the electric mixer throughout. The whole process of adding the sugar should take about 8 minutes, at the end of which you will have a very thick and silky mixture. Then add the vanilla essence and gently mix in.

4. With a tablespoon, dab three blobs of the mixture onto the baking tray and then lay over a piece of baking paper so it is held in place. Dump the meringue onto the paper in the centre of the tray and shape so you have a dip in the centre where the cream and fruit will sit. You can decide how high or low and wide to make the meringue.

5. Put the tray into the oven and immediately turn the temperature down to 130°C/250°F/gas mark 1. Leave the meringue in the oven for an hour and a half and then turn off the oven entirely. Leave the meringue to cool in the oven for another couple of hours.

6. When the meringue has cooled, carefully turn it upside down – I use another baking tray to support it as you turn – and gently peel off the paper; then turn it back onto a big plate or board. Whip up the cream – you can add a tablespoon of icing sugar if you like, but you don't need it – and spoon it into the hollow of the meringue; then pile the fruit on top.

12

HEAVY BONES

'Have you lost weight?'

I know my friends and family always mean well, but after careful observation over many years, I've worked out that the only time anyone ever asks me this question is when I know my weight has actually gone up. I can understand the thought process. If you see someone and think they look a bit bigger than the last time you saw them, you're not going to say that, but because it's on your mind, you end up lurching in the other direction. I know I should respond with a rueful smile before going straight on a diet, but, instead, I generally smile back cheerfully: 'All going in the right direction.'

I have a great line in excuses to avoid going on a diet. And it all starts with my mum. I think she was rather proud to have a chunky, bouncy, healthy child, always a stone heavier than my friends. 'He's not fat,' she would say, 'just heavy-boned.' She taught me to cook good, hearty meals, and I learned from both her and my dad to leave nothing on the plate. I also definitely inherited my love of a snack from my mum's daily routine: Jacob's cream crackers for elevenses; biscuits with tea in the afternoon; peanuts before dinner; a Bounty bar or cheese and biscuits in front of the TV in the evening; and then a mug of Ovaltine before bed.

No one seemed to worry much about healthy eating or children's diets back in the 1970s. We were taught to brush our teeth twice a day, and to cross the road safely using the Green Cross Code. The government had just ruled that wearing a seat belt in the car was a good idea and drinking alcohol while driving was not. TV advertising of cigarettes was outlawed just before I was born, and health warnings on packets followed in 1971. But our attitude to sugar back then was summed up by the famous Mars advert: 'A Mars a day helps you work, rest and play'; or the Milky Way slogan: 'The sweet you can eat between meals without ruining your appetite' – which traded on the basis that eating this particular chocolate snack wouldn't stop you eating more later.

On the fitness side of the equation, I did play lots of football and rugby at school and university. Then, when I started working full-time in my twenties, I played football twice a week, for the *Financial Times* in a London AstroTurf midweek league and at the weekend for the Hampstead Heathens in the Southern Olympian league, driving round the M25 every Saturday to play matches in suburban parks. I had a cooked breakfast before I left, and then sausages and chips with the team after the match. That was my version of healthy living, and I loved it. Sadly, my weekly football-playing rapidly tailed off when I joined the Treasury and Yvette was elected to Parliament in 1997. Travelling to and fro between Yorkshire and London every weekend made playing for a Saturday football team impossible. I did sign up for a year's membership at a Westminster gym, but I can't have gone more than three times and let it lapse.

Around my fortieth birthday, I started to notice. There comes a point in any man's life when you look at last year's holiday photos and don't recognise that slightly tubby guy standing near your wife. But, like my mum, I gave myself plenty of excuses. After all, I was heavy-boned, and I did exercise whenever I got the chance; I just didn't get the chance very often. I continued to play the odd charity football match without difficulty and chased the kids around the park at the weekend. In my mind's eye, I still had the fitness and physique of a late-era Robbie Fowler, or perhaps that football legend from my childhood, Malcolm Macdonald.

Once I made it to the Cabinet, the TV cameras and press photographers started taking more notice of me at our annual Sunday morning Labour Party Conference football match against the members of the political press. The resulting pictures of me in the *Daily Mail* and *Daily Telegraph* did reveal a little tummy spread, but I rational-ised that, while their picture desks would want to show Cristiano Ronaldo or Wayne Rooney at their most athletic, they were trying to do the opposite with me. Clearly, these carefully selected pictures didn't show the *real* me, I figured, and I just needed to be more careful during the pre-match stretching exercises.

By the time we left government in 2010, however, the mismatch between my perception of myself – fit, sleek and sporty – and the photographic reality was becoming gapingly wide. I decided I needed the solution most men try in the early phase of their mid-life crisis: sudden bouts of intense physical activity. I first turned to running marathons – or, more accurately, was completely bounced into it.

I was the guest speaker at a dinner for Whizz-Kids, a disabled children's charity, which was one of the London Marathon's early charity partners, and after my speech their CEO produced a running vest with my name on and announced, without any prior consultation, that I had agreed to run the marathon for them. The assembled donors started pledging enthusiastically and, six months later, I emerged from a state of total denial and started training. I ended up doing the marathon three years in a row, with a best time just below the magic five hours, raising £160,000 for Whizz-Kids and Action for Stammering Children in the process. That was the good news. The bad news was that I didn't lose a pound of weight in that time. If anything, I gained a little. Perhaps I was starving when I came back from a training run and overindulged. As ever, I had my mum's excuses at the ready: I was just swapping fat for muscle, leaving me now with heavy bones *and* heavy muscles.

Yvette thought *Strictly Come Dancing* might succeed

where the marathons had failed – and forty hours of energetic training in a dance studio each week for three full months did make a difference. Katya and I trained most days at a dance studio on Old Street in London. It was hard work and, by lunchtime, we were starving. We usually went to the same local Vietnamese place just round the corner – there was always a long queue and I got quite a few funny looks standing in my dance studio 'leisurewear'. But the food was great and super-healthy BBQ pork, spicy beef, soups and *banh mi* rolls with pate, chilli and coriander.

I lost over half a stone that autumn and I was so impressed with my own efforts, I made the classic mistake of having a new suit fitted just after the show ended. I then embarked on the *Strictly Come Dancing* arena tour, performing once or twice a day in front of packed, cheering audiences. The problem was we didn't need to train – we already knew the routines – and the food on the tour was incredible. The Eat to the Beat catering team travelled with us from venue to venue, wheeling their own refrigeration units, utensils and ingredients into each arena and producing amazing three course meals. It wasn't long before I had to ring the tailors to ask whether they could let out the waistband in my new suit.

Then came Kilimanjaro, an intense and exhausting experience where I could feel the strain my body was under. Once again, the food was brilliant – this time not cooked by a huge catering team, but by two guys in the mouth of a tent which they then packed up and carried from camp to camp as we climbed high into the African skies. The expedition leaders said we had to eat and drink a lot to replenish the calories we were burning, and once again, I lost over half a stone, this time in just ten days. But when we returned to London, I was shattered and spent the next three weeks exhausted, lazing around, eating the same amount as I'd done on the mountain, and was soon back where I started.

Yvette had, by this point, reached a firm conclusion. Perhaps it wasn't my fitness I needed to worry about, so much as my diet? I was sceptical, I told her. Look at my dad and my uncles – we're built to work in the fields, it's in our genes. For years, I've had on-off goes at many different low-carb diets, but never succeeded in eating less. The 5:2 diet doesn't work for me – the two low-calorie days are hellish and I more than make up for it over the course of the other five. I've tried various versions of the Dukan diet, just consuming steak, red wine and cheese, but then I persuade myself it's time to go back to something less rich and more balanced and that's the end of that. I do know that if I substitute more green vegetables for carbs, then my weight comes down, but, fundamentally, I enjoy food – and I just like bread, potatoes and pasta too much. I try and try for days at a time and then, when I'm tired and tempted, I'll just think, *What the heck*, and reach for the crisps or peanuts.

I also know that when I'm working hard and don't have time to eat proper meals, my weight goes down – but whenever I finish an intense period of work and relax, my eating ticks back up again and with it the weight. Excuses, excuses. As for alcohol, I rarely drink beer and try to have three or four days off a week. But I do like a glass of red wine, and I rationalise that if I cut out alcohol entirely, what I'd lose in calories I'd gain in stress. But I keep trying, and making excuses, and trying again. As I write this, I'm embarking on another bout of low–carb starvation. Maybe this will be the time that makes all the difference. Or else I'll need to find another extreme charity challenge.

I wonder if it's all my mum's fault that I can't manage to make dieting work for me. And not just because of the recipes she taught me to cook and her penchant for snacks that I inherited. I'm wondering whether that first roast beef and Yorkshire pudding dinner she fed me when I was just three weeks old set me on the wrong path. Yes, it was on the advice of the health visitor. And no, science hasn't found any link between eating solids when very young and finding it hard to diet in later life. But perhaps from that moment on I never had a chance. Anyway, it's the best excuse I've come up with so far.

PRAWN PHO WITH VIETNAMESE SALMON

Serves 4

I fell in love with Vietnamese cooking when I was on *Strictly*. But while I've tried to cook Vietnamese dishes at home, it's not easy to get the same light, spicy, salty tastes. My *banh mi* rolls aren't bad and the fresh spring rolls we've made at home were fine. I guess there are some cuisines that are just best cooked by the experts. I have found a couple of Vietnamese recipes that do work really well, however: a healthy, fiery soup with a wonderful aroma and deep flavours (unlike the disastrous 'rustle up' pea pho which nearly got me thrown off *Best Home Cook*, there is no shortage of flavour in this recipe); and a beautiful salmon recipe which is a big favourite of Yvette and my daughters. I leave out the honey if I'm on one of my low-carb diets.

Prawn Pho

Serves 4

INGREDIENTS

- 1 litre chicken stock
- 3 garlic cloves, peeled and sliced
- 3 stalks lemongrass, outer layer removed, bashed with a saucepan to soften and cut in half
- 3 red bird's eye chillies (2 whole, 1 finely chopped)
- 3cm piece of ginger, also bashed
- 100g beansprouts
- 100g vermicelli noodles (or 2 packs of thin or medium wok-ready noodles)
- 400g peeled tiger prawns
- 4 tbsp fish sauce
- A handful of coriander leaves
- A handful of mint leaves
- 2 limes, quartered
- A few more coriander leaves and mint to garnish

Method

1. Put the chicken stock in a heavy pan. Add the garlic, lemongrass, whole chillies, half the chopped chilli and ginger. Bring to the boil and simmer for half an hour.

2. Put the noodles into a saucepan, cover in boiling water, cook for 4 minutes and then turn off the heat. Add the prawns and fish sauce to the stock, and simmer for a further 5 minutes.

3. Turn off the heat. Remove the lemongrass, ginger and whole chillies. Add the beansprouts and handfuls of coriander and mint leaves.

4. Drain the noodles, put into bowls, ladle over the soup, sprinkle the remaining chopped chilli, mint and coriander and serve with a quarter of lime on the side.

Vietnamese Salmon

Serves 4

Ingredients

- 4 salmon fillets
- 4 garlic cloves, peeled and finely chopped

- 2 tbsp fish sauce
- 4 tbsp honey
- 2 tbsp lemon juice
- ½ tsp ground black pepper
- 2 tbsps fresh coriander, finely chopped and an extra 1 tbsp to garnish

METHOD

1. Mix the garlic, fish sauce, honey, lemon juice, black pepper and coriander in a bowl and let the salmon sit in the mixture for at least 30 minutes. Preheat the oven to 180°C/350°F/gas mark 4 and lay a large piece of tin foil across an ovenproof dish.

2. Transfer the salmon, still coated in the marinade, onto the foil and wrap it around the fish in a loose parcel to stop the marinade spilling out. Cook in the oven for 18 minutes.

3. Remove the salmon and juices to a serving dish and sprinkle over the extra tablespoon of coriander if you have any. Serve with rice and perhaps some broccoli stir-fried in some hot sesame oil with garlic, chilli and a tablespoon of soy or fish sauce until tender.

BLACK BEAN SOUP

Serves 4

My mum often made soup for Saturday lunch, usually tomato, mushroom, celery or leek. She'd sweat the vegetables slowly in butter for ten minutes, pulp them in a mixer and then blend with chicken stock, salt and pepper and some cream. If there was leftover chicken, she would dice that up and throw it in too. I often make those simple, healthy soups, especially when there are leftovers or vegetables getting near their sell-by date. Or when I'm on a diet.

But sometimes it's worth making the effort to do something more laborious. One favourite of mine is clam chowder, although it only really works if you buy fresh clams rather than using the tinned kind. My other favourite American-style soup uses black beans (dried or canned) and is also well worth the effort. The cool tomato salsa and sour cream on top offset it beautifully, and it's definitely healthy.

Ingredients

- 1 tbsp olive oil
- 2 garlic cloves, peeled and finely chopped
- 1 medium onion, peeled and finely chopped
- 1 medium carrot, diced
- 2 large green jalapeño chillies
- 1 medium glass of red wine
- 2 × 400g can black beans
- 1 litre chicken stock
- Juice of 1 lime
- Salt and pepper
- Tomato salsa (see Page 175)
- 300ml sour cream

Method

1. Heat the olive oil in a heavy pan, add the garlic, onion, carrot and chillies, and cook over a moderate heat for 7 minutes. Add the wine and let it bubble for 2 minutes.

2. Rinse the beans in a colander and add them to the pot, followed by the stock. Bring to the boil and simmer for 30 minutes.

3. Remove from the heat and add the lime juice (saving a tablespoon to mix into the sour cream), salt and pepper. Make the tomato salsa (see Page 175).

4. Ladle half of the soup into a blender and blitz for a few minutes until smooth, before adding it back into the pot and bringing the soup to a simmer.

5. Serve in bowls with a tablespoon of tomato salsa and a tablespoon of sour cream on top.

13

GROWING OLD

My parents moved back from Italy to Norfolk in 2001 and four years later we started to realise my mum's memory was becoming a problem. She was getting increasingly forgetful and we were all becoming used to having the same conversation with her again and again. She was still functioning normally, however – driving the car, doing the shopping, cooking for my dad, even coming up to London to look after our kids when we needed help. And if we ever raised mum's failing memory with her, we were crossly dismissed.

One Saturday evening the whole family was sitting around the dining-room table at my parents' north Norfolk house – Yvette, my sister and brother, their partners and the six chattering cousins. Mum had made a big chicken casserole which I carried through from the kitchen for my dad to dole out. Yvette fetched big serving spoons and my sister carried through the vegetables. We all passed round plates of steaming chicken, began to tuck in, and then, knives and forks in hand, we all stopped and looked at each other. The casserole looked fine, but when we cut into the chicken it was completely raw. The casserole should have been in the oven for at least an hour and a half, but Mum couldn't have cooked it for more than ten minutes. No one knew quite what to do, the silence awkward and painful, until my sister Joanna said breezily: 'Maybe it just needs a little bit more time in the oven', and we all cleared the plates back into the pot and reheated the oven. My mum just sat there looking bewildered.

We knew that evening that her dementia was real and getting worse. A few weeks later we were all round for dinner again and this time Mum had made lasagne – her signature dish. In fact, she had made two full dishes since there were so many of us. One of the lasagnes was perfect – my mum's lasagne at its best. But the other was a soupy mess, meat sauce and white sauce mingling but with no pasta in the dish at all. This time no one said anything. We carried on talking and laughing while Yvette subtly made sure that everyone had a little bit of pasta on their plate. And, in many different ways, we carried on saying nothing and working around Mum's emerging dementia for years after that.

Looking back, and I know it's the same for so many other families, the biggest regret is that we couldn't get Mum to acknowledge what was going on and let us talk to her about how she wanted to deal with it while there was still the chance to fully include her in that conversation and allow her some proper ownership of the situation. But at no point was she ever willing to do that, and we never felt able to push it. When we suggested notepads or noticeboards where she could make lists, she'd just dismiss us as being silly. And as the dementia progressed, she would forget what we had said anyway. She was strong, proud and private. I don't know if this was something she would ever have felt able to face up to, even to herself.

Steadily, as things became more serious, life became very hard for my mum and dad. By now, they were spending a lot of their time in a house they had rented in the centre of Norwich, which was much more practical and accessible. While we'd all seen enough depictions of dementia, or read enough accounts, to understand the impact it will have on someone's memory, I certainly didn't appreciate the extent to which it would affect my mum's moods, often making her upset and angry. My dad coped amazingly well for quite a few years, but he found it harder and harder to manage, while my mum resisted having anyone else in the house to help out. Finally, a full ten years on from those early signs, she started to try to leave home to return to her long-dead parents in another part of Norwich. When my dad locked the doors in an attempt to keep her safe, this just added to her frustration.

When we visited during those years, I saw and experienced first-hand the stress my dad dealt with every day. He had taken over doing all the cooking – mainly reheating supermarket meals – because my mum couldn't manage to cook anymore. Sometimes when we visited, we had large takeaways delivered or took our whole tribe to a local restaurant. But my dad also wanted to have the whole family in their home eating together as we had always done. At his request, I cooked my version of Mum's old lasagne recipe, and, much to my surprise, a cheese soufflé that I often cooked at home became a great favourite of my dad's, and he'd regularly request it when I rang to plan our visits.

I also took over the cooking of the Sunday lunch. For my mum, this was all very destabilising – someone else in her kitchen, using her oven, usurping her role. I had to be on my toes, because if I lost concentration for a moment, she would dart across the kitchen to open the oven and start taking things out, declaring them cooked. If I got ingredients out, she tried to put them away. And if I asked her to help by peeling vegetables, she would take offence at being given the menial tasks. If my dad came in to try to assist, and sensed the stress in the room, he'd unfortunately make things ten times worse by starting to do the washing up while I was still trying to cook.

These were extremely stressful moments, but it was increasingly tricky for my sister or brother to lure Mum out of the kitchen on some pretence. Strangely, while the dementia was increasingly bad, at the same time she could be razor sharp and ultra-resistant to any attempts to divert her attention. That kind of active, high-functioning dementia is very difficult to deal with. However hard you try to be caring, it's so easy to lose patience when someone is sharing the same space but operating on a totally different plane. I would snap, 'Stop that, Mum, they're not cooked yet'; but then feel huge and immediate remorse that I was telling her off for something she couldn't control and didn't understand. I'm sure the same thing happened to my dad again and again. He's not the most patient person, but he tried and tried. Then I would hear him say, 'I've already told you. That's not what we agreed. That's not what we decided.' Mum would become upset and he would too. A few minutes later, though, my mum had forgotten all about it while my poor dad carried the burden of those moments for hours and days afterwards.

Throughout all these more advanced stages, the doctors and experts continued to be astounded at how effective my mum was at covering up her memory loss, bluffing her way through situations where she clearly had no idea what was going on while sharply telling off any nurse or doctor who tried to prod or poke her or spoke out of turn. She was a very unusual case of a healthy and articulate and high-functioning elderly woman with very serious dementia. It eventually became clear to everyone, after much soul-searching and experimenting with different care plans, that full-time care was the only safe option, and she moved to the dementia wing of a Norwich care home.

A friend of mine was temporarily the director of Alzheimer's Research UK, and she spoke to me about the experiences she'd had with her own mother. Increasingly, she explained, you can't have any conversations about what's *going* to happen and it's even harder to have conversations about what *has* happened. Your parent will just live in the moment, and when you are with them, you must do too – just try to make every present moment as happy as possible. She told me how much her mum loved dressing up, but that when she opened the wardrobe, her mum would sometimes say crossly, 'I don't like any of these clothes.' My friend learned there was no point in having an argument; it just upset her mum when she said, 'But you chose them', or tried to persuade her that something in the cupboard was nice. Instead, she learned to just nod, shrug her shoulders and turn away. She would then wait a minute, come back and open the same wardrobe all over again. By that time, her mum had often completely changed her mind, saying with a smile, 'Oh I do like that jacket, let me try that one on.' This is the reality of coping with dementia – you just have to live with them in each moment.

Eventually, as my mum's dementia advanced, she became much calmer, giving up a little of her fight. She returned to a simpler state and would spend hours looking at old family snaps; photo-books that Yvette put together using family photos; and special dementia-suited picture books with familiar poems or phrases in big print alongside old-fashioned scenes from the 1940s and '50s. Sometimes she would talk at length about what she saw and recognised. It was deeply impressive and humbling to see how our children could sit down with their nana again and again, with the same photo-books, and chat away with her about what they were looking at, having the same conversations over and over.

Gradually those moments when my mum would talk at length became much less common, and it felt as if she was retreating, disappearing. When we all got together in a big family group, she was often very quiet, sometimes anxious and agitated, as if she didn't know who anyone was and was finding it all too noisy and bewildering. We learned, however, that far from trying to quiet things down, if one of us then broke into song – an old hymn from church or a song from a musical – Mum's face would light up and she would start to sing along, and maybe even lead the singing as she had done years ago.

Singing has always been an important part of my mum's life – she and my dad met for the first time in the church choir when they were fourteen years old. We went to church every week when I was young and belted out the hymns. At our wedding, my mum organised over twenty family members and friends to rehearse in the morning and sing Psalm 23, 'The Lord is My Shepherd', at the wedding ceremony. Even now, with much of the rest of her memory gone, her ability to remember the words of hymns and songs has remained. She can seem totally zoned out of my conversations with her, but then if I start singing 'Lord of all Hopefulness ...' or 'And Did Those Feet ...', not just the words and the tune, but also her memory and personality, all seem to come flooding back. In the old days, when the whole extended family would get together for a meal, we would sit around the table and eat, laugh and argue. Today, when Mum is there, we sit around the table and eat, laugh and sing.

We still try to take her to Norwich Cathedral when we can, for evensong or the annual carol concert. One time I was at the Sunday morning service with Mum and I smiled encouragingly each time she looked over at me. After a while, she turned to my brother on her other side and whispered loudly: 'Who is that man and why does he keep grinning at me?' Andrew just laughed.

I inherited my love of music, and especially the music of English cathedrals, from my mum and dad. I've always listened to choral evensongs to concentrate, stay calm or to relax – at work and at home. When the BBC asked me to choose a deceased hero of mine for their 'Great Lives' series on Radio 4, I chose Herbert Howells, England's greatest twentieth-century cathedral composer. Howells was a man who knew great tragedy in his life, losing his only son, Michael, to polio in 1935 aged just nine years old. Michael's death inspired Howells' greatest writing, infused with sadness and hope, perhaps the most powerful, spiritual cathedral music anyone has ever written. But he never recovered from the loss of his son, and struggled with his faith until, at the end of life, in his nineties, he told his daughter, Ursula, that he could not believe in God.

Unlike my mum and dad and brother and sister, I was never confirmed in the Church of England. I've always kept an open mind but, like Howells, I've been a lifelong agnostic who loves church music. One of the great evenings of my life was to be invited by Sir Stephen Cleobury, the master of music at King's College Cambridge and president of the Howells Society, to sit with him in the King's organ loft as he played Howells' music and hear Stephen talk about how Howells himself had sat with him many years before, as he played that same piece in the organ loft of Westminster Abbey. It was Sir Stephen's last ever visit to King's. He died from cancer just a few short weeks later, and the music and memory of Howells was a great comfort to him. It is the spirituality and optimism and hope of Howells' music that speaks to me too. I don't need to know there is a God to believe we can live good and fulfilled lives. But nor do I need to reject the idea. For both my parents, hope and belief has sustained them in their later years.

I recently had the privilege to film *Who Do You Think You Are?* for the BBC. I traced the struggles of my, to my surprise, Scottish, great-great-great grandfather on my dad's side, and my great-great-great-great grandfather on my mother's. Our family was shocked to learn of these ancestral hardships, but I know my mum, if she could understand, would be proud to know what her forebears had endured and sacrificed to make the world a better place and protect the welfare of their families.

The day after we finished filming, I sat alone in Yorkshire staring out at our garden, overwhelmed by sadness and loneliness and thoughts about mortality. I had spent a fortnight recording the obituaries of my ancestors from nearly two hundred years ago: men with families, hopes and dreams, who faced struggles and made mistakes, and will have sat around tables with their families eating, laughing, perhaps singing, and wondering what the future would bring. It's all too easy as you grow older to be haunted by the thought that you too will eventually be gone or living a shell of your former life.

Nothing really prepares you for parenthood, for your parents getting old, or for facing the realities of death and loss. But making that BBC film about our family's past drove home to me that it's in the here and now that we live our lives and make our contribution. We owe it to ourselves and each other to make the most of every day. So that day in Yorkshire, I shook myself out of it, and resolved just to enjoy every day I can, laughing with Yvette, cooking for our kids and singing with my mum, living in the moment, opening the wardrobe again each morning to take a fresh look at what's inside.

My dad has now moved permanently into the centre of Norwich, just ten minutes' drive from my mum's care home. She is safe and well and eats voraciously, wolfing down the cheese straws and sausage rolls my dad is now baking at home most days to take in to her; this in addition to a full English breakfast and a three-course lunch every day, with dishes like chicken curry or fish pie that she would not have dreamed of eating before. It remains very important to my dad to have my mum and all the family round the table for Sunday lunch. Important for him and for all of us. So I do the cooking and Mum arrives in a taxi with her carer just before the meal is served. Most of the time, she is so different to the active, sparky, arguing, caring mum we all grew up with that it's difficult to recognise her as the same person. But then, sometimes, if I make a funny face or sing a silly song, she will turn to my dad or Yvette, roll her eyes and give them the same look she's given them so many times over the years.

One unexpected bonus of my time on *Strictly* is that my mum and her carers can now watch my old dances on YouTube. Every time she watches, she's seeing them for the first time, and can't quite work out what on earth this vaguely familiar character is doing, dressed up in front of a cheering crowd, and prancing around in a check shirt, green face or blue suit. Even now, just sometimes, she will turn to her carer, shake her head, and roll her eyes: 'What on earth is he doing now?'

CHEESE AND THYME SOUFFLÉ

Serves 5

My dad has become a soufflé fan in recent years, although he doesn't want anything too fancy – just cheese is fine. This is not a dish my mum cooked, and so it's not something he would ever have eaten at home before. But he has turned out to be rather more willing to try new things than I expected, which is to say more than not at all. In recent years he has become much more adventurous in what he cooks for himself. He has bought himself a new copy of Delia's Smith's *How to Cook* and sends us fabulous photos on WhatsApp most days. But he hasn't tried making a soufflé. Yet.

This sounds such a frightening dish to attempt but it's easy to cook, looks hugely impressive and works every time. Don't worry that it won't rise – it will. And don't worry about opening the oven door to check it – once is fine if you are quick. You can substitute other strong cheeses and ditch the thyme if you prefer, or switch it for dried oregano or fresh parsley. One nice variation is to get a piece of smoked haddock, cook it for 10 minutes in the milk to release some flavour, perhaps with a bay leaf; and then put the flaked haddock at the bottom of the soufflé dish or ramekins with a teaspoon of double cream. Or you could buy a dressed crab, put a teaspoon of white crab meat in the bottom of each ramekin and then mix the rest of the white crab, along with the brown meat into the cheese sauce with the egg yolks. If using haddock or crab, I would drop the thyme from the recipe.

Ingredients

- 6 tbsp butter
- 4 tbsp finely chopped thyme
- 150g Parmesan, grated
- 4 tbsp plain flour
- 400ml whole milk
- 8 eggs
- 175g Gruyère cheese, grated
- Salt and pepper

Method

1. You will need a large soufflé dish or eight ramekins. Melt 2 tablespoons of the butter in a microwave, smear the

dish(es) with it, and use 1 teaspoon of the thyme and 2 teaspoons of the Parmesan cheese to sprinkle over the butter to form a light coating on the dish walls. Separate the eight eggs, keeping all of the whites and six of the yolks. Melt the remaining butter in a large saucepan, add the flour and whisk for a minute before slowly adding the milk, continuing to whisk as it thickens. Bring to the boil, whisking regularly, and then set aside to cool for 5 minutes. Add the six egg yolks, half of the Gruyère and remaining Parmesan cheese, the rest of the thyme and salt and pepper and whisk until smooth.

2. Preheat the oven to 180°C/350°F/gas mark 4.

3. Put the egg whites into a clean bowl and whisk with an electric mixer until they form stiff peaks – they should stand up straight when you fluff them. Transfer a third of the stiff whites into the cheesy sauce and stir them in. Pour the mixture back into the gap you've just made in the stiff whites and fold in carefully. Add the rest of the cheese and fold in carefully until fully incorporated.

4. Pour into the soufflé dish (or ramekins), put in the middle of the oven, and cook for 40 mins (25 minutes if using ramekins) until nicely risen and brown on top. Serve straight out of the oven before the soufflé even thinks about sinking.

CRAB & SAMPHIRE TART

Serves 8

The recipes we love are, of course, about taste, but they are also about memory. A particular flavour, smell or crunch can transport us to a different time and bring back so many more recollections. When we went up to Sheringham on the north Norfolk coast to visit during my childhood, my Auntie Doreen would buy beautiful Cromer crabs for tea. My Uncle Frank, the local bank manager, was also the treasurer of the local RNLI and had to rush down to the sea whenever it was called out to certify the trip and ensure the volunteer lifeboatmen were properly insured. As a result, he knew all the local fishermen, and my uncle and aunt always had the freshest lobsters and crabs. Auntie Doreen didn't go in for fancy ways with cooking and we always had crab sandwiches, rich and salty and tasting of the sea. For me, the smell of crab takes me back to my childhood, the Norfolk sea air and playing bowls in the back garden while my mum and aunt got the tea ready.

My own American cooking influences mean I like to make New England-style crab cakes, sweet and lightly fried with a pink mayonnaise. But concealing the crab among a wide range of other ingredients always seems a waste of a really good Norfolk crab. And while a simple crab salad always goes down well, this recipe for a rich tart bursts with crabby flavour. I've combined it here with another local Norfolk speciality, samphire, which grows wild along the coast and gives the tart an extra salty crunch. This recipe uses all the crab – brown meat as well as white – but whatever you do, don't call the samphire 'seaweed', because, in my experience, that guarantees the kids will refuse to eat it.

INGREDIENTS

FOR THE PASTRY:

- 165g plain flour
- Pinch of salt
- 25g lard
- 50g butter
- 1 egg, beaten
- 1 tbsp water
- 1 egg yolk, beaten

FOR THE FILLING

- 120g samphire, washed and roughly chopped
- 3 eggs

- 425ml whipping cream
- ½ tsp nutmeg
- 40g Parmesan, grated
- 1 tbsp olive oil
- 450g crabmeat, brown and white separated
- 2 bunches spring onions

METHOD

1. Preheat the oven to 170°C/325°F/gas mark 3.

2. To make the pastry, rub the butter and lard into the flour and salt until fine, add the egg and water and form into a ball. Rest in the fridge for 20 minutes and then carefully roll out and lay into a greased 25cm metal flan tin, trimming the edges. Lay baking paper over the pastry, cover it with baking beans, and put in the oven for 20 minutes. Remove the pastry from the oven, take out the baking beans, brush the pastry with egg yolk and return to the oven for a further 10 minutes.

3. While you allow the pastry case to cool a little, turn the oven up to 180°C/350°F/gas mark 4 and blanch the chopped samphire in boiling water for 5 minutes, then drain and set aside.

4. Lightly beat the eggs, cream and nutmeg. Stir in the cheese and olive oil and the white crabmeat. Smear the base of the cooling pastry case with the brown crabmeat

and sprinkle over the spring onions. Pour the crabby custard into the pastry case and then sprinkle the samphire all over and watch it sink in.

5. Put the tart in the oven for 50 minutes. It should brown and set in the middle – but still be a little wobbly.

14

FLYING THE NEST

Yvette and I approached our eldest daughter's eighteenth birthday with trepidation. Her A levels finally over, she was on the verge of becoming our first child to fly the nest.

We couldn't work out how to mark the occasion. What present would be sufficiently important or special? I was racking my brains for months. Then, a few weeks before her birthday, she told Yvette what she wanted. And it took my breath away. She asked for a cookbook with all the recipes that I'd cooked for her and the family over the past eighteen years. Something she could take away with her, use for herself in the years to come, and always help her to remember home.

I got to work. Yvette had made many photo-books over the years, but I was a novice, and this one needed text too. I wrote out all her favourite recipes, each with cooking tips and any associated family history, while Yvette searched out photos of our daughter over the years with family and friends, to make it more than a cookbook. After a week of editing, uploading the text and photos on an iPad, fiddling with fonts and margins, it was done and sent off to the printers. A few days later, three beautiful hardback books arrived – and I only found one annoying spelling mistake. I called the book 'Dishes for My Daughter', and it was the best present I've ever given.

We followed that first cookbook two years later with 'Dishes for Our Son' as he got ready to fly the nest himself. It was a rather different book, as befits our fussiest eater, with a very long final section entitled 'Things Our Son Might Eat One Day ...' I didn't know at the time whether these cookbooks would turn out to be useful, although the fact that both of our kids made a pre-university trip to Ikea with their mum to buy their own kitchen equipment was a good sign. It was only when I got photos back from them both, taken with their new university friends, sitting round in kitchens and eating one of the recipes they'd made from their cookbook, that I knew they had worked.

Our offspring leaving home is a time of great stress and challenge for us parents as well as the kids. They come and go, work, study and travel, and we learn to get used to them not being around, closing their bedroom doors to hide the truth, relying on text messages and late-night phone calls to keep in touch; and being OK with all that. We quickly discover that we are much more stressed about our kids leaving on these adventures than they are; and that the number of times they ring home will be in inverse proportion to how they are doing – extended periods of silence aren't something to worry about, we learn; they're the clearest indication that things are going well.

University departure day was nostalgic for both Yvette and me, remembering our own first nerve-racking steps into a new life. Three decades before, I had got ready to leave, sitting in our living room in Nottingham, surrounded by half-packed boxes and piles of books, watching Neil Kinnock make his famous speech to the 1985 Labour Party Conference in Bournemouth, confronting Derek Hatton and the Militant Tendency. My mum and dad drove me from Nottingham to Oxford with my bike on the roof rack, and spent a long time with me that day settling me in. I don't remember being worked up about their presence at all.

It was very different with our oldest daughter. Yvette and I were issued with strict instructions on what we were and weren't allowed to do, and injunctions to keep a low profile and not do anything that drew any attention. I suppose I had only myself to blame for that, having drawn far too much dodgy attention to myself in recent years.

The kids leaving home was stressful but, of course, we soon discovered they hadn't left for good. They were soon back for Christmas, summer holidays or just for a weekend break away from the frenetic pace of university life. And that was in normal times. When the first lockdown of 2020 came along, we suddenly had them all back again living under one roof. To have all the family home together again like that, day after day, week after week, was totally unexpected, something we never thought we would have again, and a reflection of the unprecedented times we were suddenly dealing with.

My brother and I could see the way things were going

in advance of the formal lockdown and dashed down to Norwich to check that my dad would be OK and that my mum's care home was still functioning properly and fully staffed, even if we weren't allowed to see her. We spent a couple of hours visiting local restaurants to see where my dad could carry on ordering takeaways if the lockdown meant everything else shut. He was in constant touch with my mum's carers, especially Alise, Debbie, Tina, and his hugely dependable older brother, John, who lived nearby. I was moved by the proactive kindness of his neighbours, who came round to give us their phone numbers and tell him and us that if there was anything he needed, they were there for him.

Best of all, we met Suzy, my dad's brand-new Golden Retriever, whom – by a great stroke of fortune and coincidence – he had decided to give a home to just a few weeks before. For my dad, like so many thousands more across the country, his new dog would prove a great source of comfort and companionship in the months to come, and it was a huge reassurance for me and my brother and sister that he wasn't just on his own.

As for us, our kids were safe, so my main responsibility was making sure they had enough to eat. The scenes of empty shelves in supermarkets brought back uncomfortable memories of the 2000 fuel dispute when I was at the Treasury and watched in alarm as people started queuing for hours at a time to buy petrol, panicking that supplies were about to run out, and, by doing so, guaranteeing that was exactly what started to happen. You can't blame people: it's a natural human instinct so ingrained in our behaviour that whole economic theories have been written about it. After all, how many of us have been tempted to join a growing queue, with no idea what it's for, just because other normal-looking people are doing so, and we're worried we'll regret it later if we don't? At the very least, it takes a strong will not to wander over and ask, 'What's this for?'

Our biggest worry back in the summer of 2000 was that a lack of fuel – and gridlocked roads – would start affecting other supply chains, and we'd start to see shortages of basic food supplies or medicines in the shops. That risk, coupled with the real fear that the ambulance network would start running out of fuel, helped persuade the newspapers to stop egging on the protests. They may also have been wondering what would happen when the delivery trucks at their print-works ran out of diesel. For a few days in March 2020, things felt even more serious. But – aside from some short-term shortages of toilet roll and supermarket-enforced rationing of pasta and bread – the retail supply chains held up remarkably well and returned to normal fairly quickly. Hoarding may be silly and self-defeating, but it's just human nature. I can vividly recall my own queasy feeling as I found myself – for no good reason – questioning whether I'd pressed 'confirm' on an online food delivery, only to find the website had collapsed under the weight of traffic. Fortunately, I had. But I had to 'queue' for two hours on the website to make sure.

What strange, frustrating and worrying times those were

for all of us, and infinitely worse for the hundreds of thousands who lost loved ones or had to carry on doing vital jobs in incredibly difficult and frightening conditions, from doctors, nurses and care workers to bus and lorry drivers. While Yvette still had constituency and parliamentary responsibilities, all my work ground to a halt as conferences were cancelled, a BBC series I was about to film was put on hold and my scheduled TV filming in America suddenly looked highly doubtful. I knew I had it easy, but the sudden emptiness of my diary still came as a shock. When you've always associated work with sitting down at a desk, what happens when you sit there with nothing to do?

Even my alternative workspace at home, the kitchen, suddenly felt like less of a sanctuary than normal. The boredom and monotony of lockdown affected my feelings about cooking, and I very quickly got fed up with cooking my regular recipes. I decided it was time to innovate, and for a fortnight I tried new recipes, new ingredients and new cookbooks: Korean, Malaysian, and a new recipe book specialising in oven dishes, which all gave me some new twists on familiar dishes. Soon, however, I had to give up trying – it wasn't that my new recipes didn't work, but home cooks need appreciation, and every night I was dealing with disappointment from the kids. 'What is this?', 'Is there anything else?', 'Why have you done it this way?', 'Can't you just do it like you always do?'

I was disappointed initially, but realised it was no surprise that our kids weren't warming to my innovative cooking.

Lockdown was already so weird, everyone naturally just wanted things to feel normal and familiar where they could. In the kitchen, I just had to go back to basics. If I was going to find ways to break the boredom, it wouldn't be at the expense of happy mealtimes. So, instead, I took up yoga, using a book I'd been given for Christmas, I think as a joke: *Stiff Guy Yoga: Rediscover Your Twentysomething Self in 30 Days*. It was taxing and stretching – literally – but also hugely relaxing, and I followed the online videos every day on a mat on the kitchen floor. Most days, I also went out for a run through what were relatively traffic-free, empty streets, and the colours and sights and smells of urban life felt much more vivid than they ever had before.

Every evening we all came together to have dinner and then watch a box-set on the TV. Our best discovery was the kids' choice: *Friday Night Lights*, a five-series American show about teenagers growing up in small-town Texas, and the family and friendship dynamics – and social politics – that revolve around a high-school American football team. It was escapist and compelling and gave a regular feel-good thrill without ever being schmaltzy. Then we turned to the seventeen series of *Grey's Anatomy*.

As the weeks and months passed, the uncertainty about what was going to happen seemed to get worse and worse, and the future became harder to read. We were nervous at the start about my mum, and a number of residents did later lose their lives from Covid on her dementia wing while she worryingly tested positive but remained unscathed; but her care home was on the ball with regular testing from early on and handled a very difficult situation with great professionalism. It was my dad I was more worried about in the early months. Unable to go and see my mum or have visits from us, or even wander over to the Cathedral, he was very much alone, bar Suzy the dog. My brother, sister and I started a daily Zoom call with him to make sure he was OK. He read us chapters from the book he was writing about his life with my mum. We all had a glass of wine on a Friday. I started suggesting recipes for him to try and soon he was posting photos of his culinary efforts – roast pork, celery soup, cheese straws.

When the lockdown restrictions were finally first eased in June 2020, and we were able to visit him, we sat outside in a gazebo we put up in his front garden and ate takeaway from Shiki, a local Japanese restaurant which he'd started ordering from every other day for the previous three months. My dad, a man who didn't eat pasta in Italy, who objected to unknown sauces, and liked every dish as simple as possible, had suddenly become a connoisseur of Japanese food. It was a revolution.

These were months of loneliness, hardship and suffering for many, and there was more to come. But it was also a time of great camaraderie. On those Thursday nights when everyone went out to clap the NHS and care workers, it wasn't simply the collective public gratitude which was so striking, but the fact that I'd never seen so many people out on the street waving and smiling at each other before. So when the footballer Marcus Rashford started his campaign to pressurise the government to do more to help low-income children to eat outside the school terms, he was tapping into something deep and powerful. Like many other nearby businesses, the local Magnet pub in Castleford had already organised itself to cook lunches for local children during the summer holidays. They were overwhelmed by huge donations of food from people without a lot themselves but who wanted to do more. That outpouring of generosity was repeated in cities, towns and villages across the UK. A collective determination to tackle food poverty and support people in hardship, which had been building in recent years with the growth of food banks, suddenly crystallised in the lockdown.

When the restrictions eased later that summer – temporarily as it turned out – it was such a relief that our two oldest kids could plan to go back to university. They were desperate for some freedom by then, and we were desperate for them to escape this unnatural torture for a teenager of being forcibly cooped up at home. Two nights before we dropped my son off for his first term at university, I woke up in a cold sweat at 3 a.m., not concerned about him flying the nest, but worrying about what would happen if Yvette or I got Covid symptoms which meant he couldn't go.

My work also started to pick up again. In July we managed to complete the *Who Do You Think You Are?* shoot that had been cancelled in the first weeks of the lockdown back in March. And then a call came through asking if I'd like to take part in a new lockdown-inspired BBC production, *Celebrity Best Home Cook*. Well, I thought, I'd been practising all summer, and preparing all my life. Time to pull on an apron and have a go.

I didn't know until weeks later quite how sceptical our kids were about me signing up to *Best Home Cook*. '*Strictly* was fine,' they told Yvette, 'because we all knew Dad couldn't dance. But he's good at cooking and he really cares. If the judges criticise what he makes, he'll get so upset.' They shook their heads. 'You shouldn't have let him do it, Mum.' I will admit my first reaction when Yvette told me this was to be a little bit offended at their brutal assessment of my dance abilities. But the kids were right. I didn't mind a jot what Craig or Bruno thought about my foot swivel or hand shape, but I did care what Mary Berry and Angela Hartnett, whose recipes I had used so many times before, would think about my cooking.

As ever, Yvette rationalised it for me. 'It wasn't dancing flair or talent that kept you in *Strictly*,' she said, 'but your willingness to have a go, to throw yourself off the deep end and not to be too worried if it all went wrong.' That's why these days, walking through the centre of Pontefract, she is often stopped, by women and men alike, who, with a chuckle and a shake of the head, say, 'Saw him on the telly again. What's he up to now?' – the same question my mum would occasionally ask her carer in the home when they'd watch videos of my old *Strictly* dances. 'But with cooking,' Yvette said, 'you really do care. You don't just want to have a go and make people laugh.' And I knew she was right. I wanted my cooking to be good. And deep down, if I couldn't exactly make my mum proud anymore, I at least wanted to do her proud.

CHICKEN NOODLE SOUP

Serves 5

This is the recipe that my oldest daughter chose for her last dinner at home before going off to university. It's an Asian-style chicken noodle soup made with whole garlic cloves, ginger, soy and – the magic ingredient – tamarind. It's always been her favourite comfort food and I made an extra-large batch so that she could take a Tupperware box away with her the next day. It tastes and smells amazing, and I find that once you've served the soup, you can always add some hot water and extra coriander to refresh what's left for second helpings or lunch the next day.

Ingredients

- 3 skinned chicken breasts
- 4 tbsp sesame oil
- 20 whole unpeeled garlic cloves
- 4 garlic cloves, peeled and finely chopped
- 1 large onion, peeled and finely chopped
- 2 carrots, chopped
- 3cm piece of ginger, peeled and grated
- 1 red chilli, finely chopped
- 1 litre chicken stock
- 100g jar tamarind paste
- 500ml water
- 4 tbsp soy sauce
- 3 packs ready-cooked medium/thick noodles
- A big handful of finely chopped coriander

Method

1. Preheat the oven to 180°C/350°F/gas mark 4.

2. Halve the chicken breasts, toss them in an ovenproof dish with the whole garlic cloves and 3 tablespoons of the sesame oil and then cook in the oven for 25 minutes.

3. Separate out the garlic cloves from the chicken and set aside; reserve the chicken juices; cut the chicken into smaller, bite-sized pieces and set aside.

4. Transfer the remaining sesame oil, plus the chicken juices, to a heavy pan, add the chopped garlic, onion, carrot, ginger and chilli and sweat on a low heat for 10 minutes until soft. Add the chicken stock, water, cooked garlic cloves and the tamarind and bring to the boil.

5. Add the chicken pieces and soy and simmer for 5 minutes before adding the noodles. Simmer for a further 5 minutes until cooked.

6. Ladle into bowls, and sprinkle with a generous covering of coriander.

BANANA BREAD

Serves 10

Like many people, I turned to bread-making and baking for comfort during the weird times we all lived through after the pandemic took hold. And, as many people discovered, there is no comfort food quite like banana bread for soothing the soul. I've experimented with many different versions over the years, and this is my favourite. It delivers a rich taste and a moist texture, bursting with banana flavour. You can make a single loaf or individual muffins in paper cases, as I did on *Sport Relief Bake Off* back in 2016.

I used spelt flour, which intrigued Paul Hollywood, but he was disgusted when I couldn't give him a good reason for it, other than seeing it recommended elsewhere. I did my research after that and found that the spelt keeps the banana bread light as well as rich, but, in truth, you could easily substitute plain flour without noticing too much difference. On *Best Home Cook*, Chris Bavin said it was the best banana bread he had ever tasted, and it became a lockdown favourite in our house. If you make muffins rather than a loaf, don't forget to halve the cooking time.

Ingredients

- 280g spelt flour – white or wholemeal
- 60g raisins (or sultanas or chopped walnuts or pecans)
- 180ml vegetable oil
- 250g dark brown sugar
- 1 ½ tsp vanilla essence
- 3 eggs
- 425g ripe bananas, skinned
- 75g natural yoghurt
- 1 ¼ tsp baking powder
- 1 ¼ tsp bicarbonate of soda
- ¾ tsp ground cinnamon
- 1 ½ tsp salt
- Half a banana and some caster sugar

For the cream cheese icing (optional)

- 200g full-fat cream cheese
- 100g icing sugar, sifted
- 1tsp cornflour
- 75ml double cream
- Half a banana
- Grated chocolate

Method

1. Preheat the oven to 170°C/325°F/gas mark 3 and line and butter a 900g loaf tin or set out 18 paper muffin cases.

2. Sieve the flour into a bowl and add the raisins. In a second bowl, whisk together the oil, sugar, vanilla and eggs. In a third bowl, mash the bananas, add the yoghurt and then mix in the baking powder, bicarbonate of soda, cinnamon and salt.

3. Combine the two wet mixtures and then add the sieved flour and the raisins and stir lightly until just combined. Pour into the tin or muffin cases.

4. If you have another banana, halve it lengthways and lay one half carefully on top of the mixture. Sprinkle with caster sugar and bake for at least 50 minutes (25 minutes if making muffins), until a knife comes out clean.

5. To make the icing, whisk all the ingredients together in a large bowl until creamy and smooth, with soft peaks formed. Spread over the top of the cake or muffins in billowing waves.

6. If you have a blowtorch, you can sprinkle sugar over the other half a banana and hold the flame until the sugar has caramelised. Carefully lay the banana on the cream cheese and sprinkle over a little grated chocolate.

Chapter 15

CHRISTMAS COOKING

I have a strong and very visceral fear of rats. Just the thought of one makes my flesh crawl. Visiting my dad's laboratory at the University of East Anglia, aged four, I poked my finger into a cage and was bitten by a white lab rat. Good for the rat, some will say. Later, as a child, moving bales of straw with my friend and his grandad at the farm next door to our house in Norfolk, a large brown rat ran out and scurried across the farmyard and I jumped out of my skin. Childhood frights which have left deep scars.

A few years ago, we arrived back on Christmas Eve having spent the weekend with my mum and dad in Norwich. Yvette's parents were already there, her mum getting everything ready for arriving family, her dad stowing provisions he had bought and cooked. Our fridge wasn't big enough to accommodate everything, so Tony had brought a cool box, which he put outside in the garden. He opened the backdoor to show me what was in there, at which point a huge brown rat jumped over his feet, ran into our kitchen and disappeared under the cupboards.

There was a rat in our kitchen and I didn't know what to do. Yvette says I went white, grabbed my coat and left the house without saying a word. How was I expected to react? I had to cook the Christmas dinner with a rat lurking somewhere near my feet, poised to jump out at any point. As nightmares went, that was close to the top of my list, and the idea that I'd be carrying scalding-hot trays and pots around the kitchen while scared out of my wits sounded like something from the opening scenes of *Casualty*.

I joined the long queue at the butcher to collect our turkey and goose in a state of shock and trauma, while, back home, Yvette knew she had a crisis on her hands. She was less bothered about the rat, and more about the prospect that – for the first time in twenty years, if we didn't get this sorted out – she might have to cook the Christmas dinner herself. Adrenalin now surging, she grabbed the Yellow Pages and started searching. After a few failed calls and answering machines – it was Christmas Eve after all – she miraculously found a local rat man who turned up an hour later. He searched hard but the built-in kitchen cupboards meant there were plenty of places for the creature to hide. He laid traps and said he would come back the day after Boxing Day, given there was nothing else he could sensibly do. We could, he said, put sticky strips across the floor in case the rat came out later that night. But he explained that the caustic glue in the strips would result in a long, slow and painful death, one which we might need to finish off ourselves. Yvette briefly considered the prospect of the children coming down in the early hours looking for evidence that Father Christmas had eaten his mince pies and instead finding a rat in the agonising final stages of life, and agreed that this was too horrific to contemplate.

I was by now sitting outside the house in the car waiting for Yvette to let me know whether it was safe to come back in. She came out to tell me the good and bad news. A ratcatcher had been and there was now a plan in place. But we did have an extra guest for Christmas and there was nothing we could do about it. The next forty-eight hours were every bit the nightmare I imagined. Every cupboard I delved into, every drawer I opened, every shopping bag I moved aside, I was expecting the rat to jump out and bite me. From Christmas Eve through to Boxing Day, as I stirred and whisked and weighed, I could feel the rat's eyes watching my every move, waiting for its chance. Even now I feel sick just thinking about it. The rat man came back the day after Boxing Day and revealed that the traps had done their job. It turned out that the rat wasn't quite the giant mutant-fanged beast of my imagination, but a rather small, scrawny thing. The ratcatcher said the poor thing would have been scared to death in our kitchen. 'Not as scared as me,' I replied. He laughed, thinking I was joking.

That dreadful Christmas is burned in my memory. Because of our uninvited guest, yes, but as much because the rat threw a massive spanner in the works on the one day of the year which should always be the same. I like a challenge, to do new things and meet new people, including inviting friends or neighbours and their families round for Christmas drinks. But Christmas Day is all about tradition, nostalgia, food and family. And rats in the kitchen have no part in any of that.

Every family has its rituals and routines on special days of the year. Yvette was surprised when she first learned that in our family we throw raw eggs over the house every Easter Sunday and try to catch them. She was even more baffled to learn that, every year, without fail since the arrival of the video recorder, my mum and dad have watched *Where Eagles Dare* on Christmas afternoon, a 1960s war film with Richard Burton in which he and his American compatriots pose as German soldiers to execute a daring rescue from a castle on a steep mountain. Every year we listened to Richard Burton, explain who was spying on who at the end. I still can't keep track of it all to this day.

My mum always ran her Christmas cooking with military precision. She made a Christmas cake every November, just like her own mum had. However many relatives came to visit, though, there was always still at least half of it left over at twelfth night, alongside the lonely yellow toffies rattling around in the otherwise empty Quality Street tin. A few days before Christmas, it was time to bake – she was a big fan of mince pies and sausage rolls. Then, on Christmas morning, and after Father Christmas had visited overnight to fill our pillowcases, my dad insisted we had a full English breakfast and that all the plates were cleared away before we opened the presents under the tree. We then dashed to church before returning to the familiar smell of a big roast chicken for the main Christmas Day course, back in the days when – for a family like ours – chicken was considered an expensive treat. We did have a Norfolk turkey once, but it was dry and there was just too much of it. I say too much, but, of course, just a couple of hours after we'd finished that enormous dinner, it was time to set out the Christmas tea as we watched *Where Eagles Dare*. Baked ham and pork pie, sausage rolls and cheese, stollen and sponge cakes, and perhaps a trifle too.

Above all, I learned from my mum not to treat Christmas lunch as a chore, but as a performance: one you prepare for weeks in advance and deliver with bravado on the day – every home cook's moment of maximum enjoyment, excitement and prowess. A family meal which, at least once a year, can extend long into the afternoon and evening without the kids rushing off to finish homework, watch a programme or just escape their parents.

One of the great challenges of life when you get together with a partner and have children is how to meld those respective traditions so that everyone is happy and, in my case, you don't upset your mother-in-law too much. Indeed, it's one of the great fascinations of life for me that every new family has these tremendous and often tense negotiations before a child's first Christmas about what traditions to establish as their own even while the tiny infant has no idea at all what any of it means.

For us, there were heated debates about whether the kids should leave out a stocking or a pillowcase, and once that was decided, whether Father Christmas would leave their main present there, or down in the sitting room by the tree. We agreed on the essential, traditional staples of the kids' stocking/pillowcase presents: a satsuma and nuts of course, and also a Terry's chocolate orange. But could Father Christmas's presents be opened whenever the kids woke up, however early, or should they have to wait until their parents were awake too? Must the Christmas English breakfast be eaten and washed up before the present-giving starts (my inherited obsession), or could it wait? And when it comes to handing out the presents, is it a free-for-all (as my mother-in-law prefers), or are they opened one by one with everyone else watching, as I would prefer but have never actually experienced as an adult?

When it comes to the kitchen, however, there is no compromise. You can only have one person in charge, and they must call all the shots. And, for the first fifteen years after our children were born, much as I was itching to try my hand at a Christmas dinner, that person wasn't me. In those years, we alternated between visiting mine and Yvette's parents. It was confusing for the kids that the order of events changed subtly year by year, but they coped. Yvette and I were always so exhausted from work back then, as well as the usual crazy last-minute Christmas Eve shopping trip, that we just wanted to collapse. My usual routine of eating a big meal, then falling asleep, would come on even more quickly than usual.

Once my mum's dementia became more serious, however, and after Yvette's parents had downsized, we started to take over the hosting and, while Yvette decorated the house, the job of Christmas cooking fell to me. I love cooking the Christmas dinner: the most important meal of the year, as much a logistical feat as a culinary challenge, especially if the wider extended family is visiting. Deciding when to do the shopping; where to put everything; how to clear room in the fridge; when to start preparing different items and courses; which jobs to trust to which kids; what each pot, hob, tray and oven need to be doing, and when, over several hours; how to get everyone sat round one table; and bringing the whole extravaganza together at exactly the right time is an organisational achievement which should ideally be done so smoothly that everyone present takes it for granted, which they inevitably will – unless it ever goes wrong.

For the home cook on Christmas Day, there are two vital tasks above all: getting everything cooked in the right order in big enough quantities on time; and not getting too drunk too early to finish the job. So, first drink in hand, while the kids play with their new toys and the adults go for a pre-dinner walk, I get down to business.

Yvette always wants a traditional roast turkey, but only on Christmas Day and perhaps the day after, which makes buying a big turkey extravagant and wasteful. I've settled on cooking both a goose and a turkey crown (which the butcher is never happy about, probably because it's harder for him to sell the legs). But it means it doesn't linger around for days. There is, of course, no room in the oven for both turkey and goose, and the first year I let the cooked goose rest for a full three hours while the turkey cooked, which wasn't ideal. But we now have a big, covered kettle BBQ which is good for slow goose cooking as it's much easier to manage the enormous quantities of fat that run off.

One extra advantage of combining turkey and goose is that, while the goose delivers the stuffing the turkey provides the gravy, ideally with some cranberry sauce on the side. I did cook a combination of turkey and beef one year, but that meant two different types of gravy on the plate at the same time, which Yvette said was much too confusing, and a little distressing for the 'fussy eaters' in the family when the two gravies started to merge. Incidentally, I know that my son – and my dad for that matter – get very irked at the suggestion that they are fussy eaters, when as far as they're concerned, their eating preferences are the opposite of fussy: they know what they like and don't want any unexpected ingredients. What they don't understand is that this is precisely the cook's nightmare when having to make a meal – at least one with any flavour in it – for a large group.

As for vegetables, it's traditional to cook lots of different types and to get all fancy – bacon with the brussels sprouts, maple syrup with parsnips, carrots in orange and so on – but I think the vegetables are there to compliment the meat and not be a distraction. Sometimes I bow to pressure and tart up the parsnips. But, frankly, I think it just messes things up and detracts from the roast potatoes, especially if you are using some of the goose fat to make them even more tasty. After the main course, we douse the Christmas pudding – mixed and pre-steamed every year in late November – in brandy and allow a slightly out-of-control fire to blaze in our kitchen for a minute or two. Yvette insists on custard with it; I prefer cream or brandy butter, which I traditionally forget until the last minute and whisk up in a hurry as the pudding blazes away.

Finally it's time to collapse in front of the TV. In the spirit of continuity with judicious innovation, our Christmas TV rituals have evolved somewhat. These days we don't watch all of *Where Eagles Dare*, just the final bus-ride escape to check if they all make it out alive, and Richard Burton's explanation on the plane to see if I follow it all this time. Instead we like a bit of Christmas post-war nostalgia – *White Christmas* or *Some Like It Hot*. As the afternoon turns to evening, we'll watch the *Strictly* Christmas special and Yvette and the kids will watch *Doctor Who* – usually my chance for a quick snooze before I get the Christmas tea ready. Then the arguments begin about the evening's entertainment – some demanding more TV and films; others a game, preferably charades. It all depends on where we are and which family is in the majority, and after twenty years as a combined family, it's good that we still have a few unresolved and rolling disputes, with all voices counting equally, except, of course, in the kitchen.

The Christmas of 2020 was hard for everyone, precisely because there were so few voices around the table compared to normal, and one in particular that I miss most of all. The last time my mum came to our house was back in 2017, the Christmas before she went into her care home. We bought a large piece of plywood to lay across our kitchen table and draped over it many metres of John Lewis' best Christmassy material to pass as a tablecloth. We squeezed twenty-four of us around that improvised table, on chairs, benches and deckchairs from the garden. I cooked a smoked salmon mousse, twenty-four individual cheese soufflés, and then roast goose and a turkey crown with all the vegetables, followed by Christmas pudding with a choice of custard or cream.

Even though it was a very different menu from the Christmas lunches she cooked when I was young, my mum tucked in approvingly and heartily – her appetite being the one thing she has never lost. And after dinner, because Mum was with us, there was no dispute about the entertainment. We began roaring out the hymns and songs we all know off by heart, with my mum beaming away as she sang along. I hadn't seen her looking so happy for a very long time.

GOOSE WITH PRUNES & BRANDY

Serves 8

My favourite Christmas goose recipe is adapted from a famous Delia Smith creation, with apple, prune and sausage stuffing. Delia suggests soaking the prunes in Armagnac, which feels like a terrible waste, and cooking two types of stuffing, which feels like too much hard work; so I do one stuffing and use ordinary brandy, which does just as well and can double up in the Christmas pudding and brandy butter too.

Ingredients

- 1 large goose, with excess fat cut off and scooped out
- Salt and pepper

For the prunes in brandy

- 150g dried prunes
- 100ml brandy
- 50g caster sugar

For the sausage and apple stuffing

- 6 large Bramley cooking apples
- 350g sausage meat
- 1 onion, peeled and finely chopped
- 50g freshly made white breadcrumbs
- 250g dried prunes, chopped
- 3 tbsp brandy
- ½ tsp ground cloves
- ½ tsp ground mace
- ½ tsp salt
- ½ tsp ground black pepper

Method

1. For the prunes in brandy, put the prunes in a saucepan with the sugar and just enough water to cover them. Simmer for 15 minutes and then drain, pour over the brandy and leave them to soak.

2. For the stuffing, mix all the ingredients together and leave for an hour to mingle.

3. Preheat the oven – or kettle BBQ – to 220°C/425°F/gas mark 7.

4. Put the stuffing in the neck end and main body of the goose. You will need metal skewers or sharp cocktail sticks to pierce and hold down the flaps and keep the stuffing in place – the more the better, as you don't want the stuffing spilling out.

5. Season the goose with salt and pepper and put into a big baking tray. If using a BBQ, I would put it in a big disposable tin foil tray. You may need to remove the goose to pour off some of the fat during cooking, so do work out how you will be able to do that in advance while things are still cool.

6. Cook the goose for half an hour and then reduce the heat down to 180°C/350°F/gas mark 4 – or lower if you want go slower. Cook a 5kg goose for a further three hours, subtracting or adding 30 minutes for each kilo difference. Rest the goose for a good half an hour before removing the stuffing and then carving carefully.

CHRISTMAS PUDDING

Serves 8

Over the years I've tried a range of seasonal starters on Christmas Day, all with the common aim that it should be fancy and flavourful, but light rather than heavy. I tried a chestnut risotto, but it was much too filling. A turkey and ham tureen looked fabulous but was a bit dull and anticipated the main course too much. My current favourite starter combination is Mary Berry's recipe for a sumptuous salmon and asparagus terrine; followed by individual soufflés, either cheese or crab.

The terrine can be made days before kept in the fridge and cut into thick slices an hour before serving. You can also prepare the components of the soufflés in advance. I find that the time it takes to eat the soufflé is also precisely the time it takes to cook the Yorkshire puddings, making sure they come fresh out of the oven for the main course.

I make individual cheese soufflés if my dad is coming and wants something plain; crab and Gruyère soufflés if not. I know people panic about soufflés, but I've always found them easy and reliable. You can get most of the work done well in advance, even the day before, just leaving the final whisking of the egg whites until the last minute.

As for the Christmas pudding, mixing the ingredients in late November and dropping 20p pieces wrapped in tin foil into the batter is the moment I know Christmas is just round the corner. After much experimentation, scouring the BBC Food website in search of inspiration, I've finally settled on my favourite pudding recipe – not dark and heavy like a Christmas cake, but light, moist and spongy. Rich but not overwhelming. It's just a pity everyone's always too full to eat it.

INGREDIENTS

- 140g sultanas
- 175g raisins
- 50g dried figs, chopped
- 60g dried apricots, chopped
- 80g glace cherries, halved
- 100ml brandy
- 50g ginger in syrup, chopped, and 1 tbsp of the syrup
- 1 large apple, grated
- 1 large orange, juice and zest
- 3 eggs
- 125g shredded suet, beef or vegetarian
- 180g soft brown sugar
- 125g fresh breadcrumbs

- 90g self-raising flour
- 1 tsp mixed spice
- 3 20p pieces, wrapped in foil if you like

Method

1. Soak the dried fruit in the brandy overnight.

2. Mix the ginger, syrup, apple, orange juice and zest. Beat the eggs and add them to the suet, sugar, breadcrumbs, flour and spice. Stir in the fruit and brandy and mix very well – the whole family can join in.

3. Grease a heatproof 1½ litre bowl. I use glass but plastic is also fine. If you don't have a lid, then find a small plate which fits. Pour the mixture into the bowl and drop in the 20p pieces.

4. Cut a circle of baking paper, using the lid or plate, and lay over the top of the pudding mixture. Place the lid or plate on top and wrap everything tightly together with a few layers of tin foil.

5. Steam the pudding in bolling water for 3½ hours. You will need a large pot with a lid. Make sure you put something in the bottom of the pot to stand the bowl on – I use an old ramekin.

6. Once the pudding has cooled, remove the foil, lid and baking paper. Wrap tightly with cling film and put aside to rest until Christmas.

7. On Christmas Day, remove the cling film, wrap securely with tin foil and steam for another 3½ hours. Flame with brandy and serve with custard, cream or brandy butter.

Conclusion

MY LIFE ON A PLATE

I normally get my instructions from our kids by text these days. A few days before the two students are due home from university, the messages arrive like clockwork. 'Can u pk me up Saturday Noon. Rst chicken Sunday.' I admit I slightly object to being the family taxi driver – I'm sure, when I was their age, I just got the train. But I don't say anything. Because the pre-order for Sunday lunch makes my heart sing. They're coming home.

I so wish I could properly tell my mum how much her teaching has made a difference to my life; and that I realise now she taught me something much more important than recipes. With my dad, she showed me how mealtimes can support and nurture family appetites in a way that goes way beyond food. When I was a kid, the main appeal of Sunday lunch was the food itself. But today I hugely value our family being together for Sunday dinner, eating, talking and laughing. And I know now how much that makes me my parents' son. The world has changed so much, and society's expectations of parenting are hugely different; and yet in both small and significant ways, so many of us still turn out like our mums and dads.

When I started a family of my own, cooking straight away became one of the most important and constant things about being a dad to our three kids. Sunday dinner is our most sacred family meal of the week, the one no one is allowed to skip, the meal our two older kids at university are always keen to come back for. These days we always have a little more gravy than we need, but I still always keep a close eye on the gravy boat. And Yvette says anyone turning up late for Sunday dinner is the one thing that's guaranteed to make me grumpy.

I'm proud I've been able to carry on into a new generation the lessons I learned from my parents. And I'm glad that I grew up at a time when that was possible. It might not have been if I'd been part of my dad's generation, and certainly wouldn't have been expected. Back then, men were often professional chefs, but rarely home cooks, and they played much less of a role in bringing up the children than fathers do today. Every change we've had on that front has been for the better, and I'm so grateful that it was my age group – and my kids – that got to enjoy the benefits.

Looking back, I can see that most of my most formative experiences and memories growing up revolved around food. And I know that doesn't make me special or unusual. On *Best Home Cook*, it was striking how much, for all of us contestants, family was the driving force behind the food we love to cook. When Shobna, Rachel and I talked about our mothers, now all challenged by dementia or other illness, we saw how much we were doing this show as a homage to them, our culinary inspirations. Karim, Desiree, Tom and Ferne talked passionately about the recipes they had learned from theirs mothers. Ruth cooked her showcase ham, egg and chips the way her dad would want and expect, with a pineapple ring on top. Ed was clearly burdened by the powerful culinary influence of his mother in law, Gareth bubblingly excited to cook for his husband. For all the very different traditions and cultures and cuisines that we each brought to the studio, the power of good food to bring people together, and allow us to demonstrate the pride we felt in our families and communities was a common bond between us all.

Despite my very English upbringing, my parents' experiences abroad in the 1960s introduced a range of different culinary influences into our home and affected my cooking from the outset. During my adult life, I've been lucky enough to travel to every continent – and invariably returned with new dishes to imitate and new cookbooks to help me, bringing a very international feel to what I cook. That has all happened over fifty years when the range of ingredients in our shops and the choice of restaurants in our high streets has also changed beyond recognition. And, of course, that transformation is not confined to food. From the TV stars we watch, the football players we support, the neighbours on our street, the colleagues we work with, and the NHS staff who look after us, our country has become so much more diverse since I was born, with people and cultural influences from around the world touching all our lives every day.

For me, the Britain we live in today is exciting and enriching and – at our best and when we choose – hugely and happily united around our common joys, our treasured institutions, and our shared sources of pride. And I believe a major part of that is the way we embrace different people and cultures and cuisines and make them our own. After all, who would want to return to a Britain without Bruno Tonioli, Jurgen Klopp or Nando's – let alone a pot of tea. How dull that would be. How un-British that would feel.

What I cook at home intertwines with these global influences every day. But so many of the tasty, fiery international dishes I cook start from the base recipes my mum taught me – I just added the chilli and spice. Like so much of what my family enjoys doing together today, it's been inherited and adapted from the home I grew up in, and the way my parents raised me. Roast dinners on Sunday, choral music on the radio, pillowcases at Christmas, supporting Norwich at Carrow Road, throwing raw eggs over the house on Easter Sunday, watching the Saturday night British Legion Remembrance Service from the Royal Albert Hall, laughing at Eurovision, singing along to the Last Night of the Proms.

My upbringing is where my identity begins and, as my parents returned to live in Norwich, as I researched the stories of my Norfolk ancestors for television, and as I reflected on my more recent family history for this book, I've become more conscious than ever of the roots and traditions that have shaped my life, and more grateful than ever to my mum and dad for passing those on to me. I see my parents in myself so much now, right down to the face that looks back at me in the mirror, but above everything – my cooking, my music, my football, my politics and my values – I see it in my feelings towards my own children, and the depths of love, hope and pride they inspire in me as I watch them go out into the world.

We all want our children to have a better future, to see the world, have amazing new experiences and, above all, to be happy. I want all that for my children, but I also want them to be proud, as I am, of where they come from. To cherish the traditions I inherited and nurtured and passed on to them. To appreciate the struggles and contributions of those who came before, and to seize their opportunities to write new and exciting chapters in that family history. I have tried hard to pass on to them the recipes and traditions which have shaped my life and the lives of those who came before me. I have done so in the full knowledge that some of these recipes and traditions will change, some will be ditched and new ones will be added too.

Most of all, I hope our kids will keep coming home. And that in their coming decades, laughter, appetite, debate and celebration will be interlaced and intertwined with shepherd's pie, lasagne and roast beef.

ROAST CHICKEN WITH LEMON & CORIANDER

Serves 6

Our Week 3 challenge on *Best Home Cook* was to make a Sunday roast dinner. I had thought I would do roast beef and Yorkshire puddings, but Yvette and the kids were clear – it had to be my roast chicken with lemon and coriander, which they regard as more of a personal specialty of mine. I was nervous about cooking for Mary Berry – who wouldn't be? – but this week I thought I was on safe ground. I'd done this roast chicken so many times before and it always tasted good. And, for an extra flourish, I would also do Yorkshire puddings, as I did every week at home.

We generally like gravy dark in our house, but when I did my usual roast chicken at home the Sunday before, Yvette wasn't sure this was the best plan. 'I know it's really good,' she said, 'but I think Mary will prefer a lighter gravy.' The kids looked at each other, none too sure. If they'd been clear about one thing during lockdown, it was that they didn't like me cooking things differently.

In the studio the next day, I spent two hours making sure my roasting tin didn't get too hot and start to caramelise the chicken juices, onion and white wine. My gravy was light and garlicky and lemony – just as Yvette thought it should be. I carried my finished roast chicken with all the trimmings up for the judging, feeling upbeat. And then it all went wrong. 'It's not really a gravy,' Angela Hartnett reflected. 'It's more of a sauce.' Mary nodded and my heart sank. 'I prefer a darker gravy,' she agreed. I couldn't believe it – the chicken was exquisite, my Yorkshire puddings were a delight, the roast potatoes were perfect, but what did that matter? I'd always said a roast lunch lives and dies by the gravy, and my trademark dish – my family inheritance – had just dropped dead on national TV. Poor Yvette was mortified when I got home that night. 'It's not your fault,' I said unconvincingly. She vowed not to give any more cooking advice until the end of the show. The kids just shook their heads and said, 'We told you so.'

Oh well. We live and learn, and at least it reminded me of those two essential lessons for the home cook: there's only one person in charge in the kitchen; and familiarity is always your best friend. And maybe one more on this occasion: trust the sound judgement and good taste of your kids; after all, they hopefully got both from you.

INGREDIENTS

- 1 large chicken
- Salt
- 2 onions, peeled and halved
- 1 lemon, halved
- 1 whole bulb of garlic, halved across the middle
- A bunch of fresh coriander (you can also use tarragon or parsley)
- 3 rashers of unsmoked bacon
- Pepper
- 1 large glass of dry white wine (not essential but recommended for the gravy)
- 1 tbsp plain flour
- 500ml water or chicken stock

METHOD

1. Turn the oven on to 200°C/400°F/gas mark 6.

2. Untie the chicken and remove the string/elastic. If there is a large lump of fat in the cavity, remove it and then rub salt all over the skin and place in a large roasting tin. Put two onion halves in the cavity and two in the tin. Squeeze the lemon halves all over the chicken and stuff in the cavity, followed by one half of the garlic bulb.

3. Peel and dice the rest of the garlic cloves and slide some under the skin of the breast and into the leg joints by piercing the skin with a knife. Put the bunch of coriander stalks in the cavity and chopped coriander under the breast skin with some garlic. Lay a rasher of bacon on each leg and a rolled-up rasher in the cavity. Pour a slug of olive oil over the breast, grind on plenty of black pepper and then pour the wine into the tin.

4. Put in the oven and cook for 30 minutes, then turn the oven down to 180°C/350°F/gas mark 4 and cook for a further 1 hour. For extra flavour and heavy-boned appetites, I often throw a dozen chipolata sausages into the tin for the final 25 minutes.

5. I usually remove the chicken to rest and carve and make the gravy in the tin using either chicken stock or the water the vegetables are cooked in. Pour off the fat from the top of the juices in the pan, stir in the flour and add the water or stock and stir as it comes to the boil and thickens. Alternatively, let the chicken rest for ten minutes and then carve into the tin. There will be less gravy, so my dad would not be happy, but the flavour is a little stronger.

Acknowledgements

Cooking, food shopping and family meals have been a big part of my daily life for decades now, though at no point did I ever expect to write a book about it. But I've learned over the last few years to embrace what life throws at you with open arms, and always to be grateful for the love and support of colleagues, friends and family. So this is my chance to say thank-you.

Credit where credit is due: the inspiration for this book came from my oldest daughter, who had the lovely and unexpected idea of asking for a collection of our family recipes for her 18th birthday. I loved putting her photobook together, writing out the ingredients, choosing the images and thinking about all the times our family had sat down to eat together. It was a true labour of love and the same was true with our son's 18th birthday book. Our younger daughter's is now in preparation.

But it was Covid-19 which turned these recipes from a private family affair into something more public. I was due to spend the summer of 2020 in the USA, tracking down Trumpland voters for the BBC. When all such travel ground to a halt, my brilliant and innovative broadcasting agent – and now my good friend, the wonderful Joanna Kaye – came up with an alternative plan. 'You like to cook, don't you?', she asked me on the phone, one Monday morning. 'Fancy a few weeks in the kitchen with Mary Berry?'

We had such fun making *Celebrity Best Home Cook*. And what a surprise it was – for all of us I think – to discover quite how much recipes and flavours were intertwined with family, memories and identity. Huge thanks to Tom, Rachel, Ferne, Shobna, Ed, Karim, Ruth, Gareth and Desiree; and to Claudia, Mary, Angela, Chris and the whole production team. Winning was quite a surprise; and then the brilliant and innovative Holly Harris at Simon & Schuster came up with the lovely idea of using the recipes to tell a bigger story of family and how the pandemic had affected us all. Appetite was born.

I can't thank Holly enough for her insight and her brilliant editing – none of this would have happened without her. Thanks also to Sophia Akhtar and Rebecca McCarthy for steering us through the production process, Jill Tytherleigh for her lovely illustrations and to my long-time collaborator and friend, Julie McCandless, for transcribing my audio files and commenting as she typed. As the manuscript came together, I had detailed comments, suggestions – and deletions – from Phil Webster, Jo Coles, Damian McBride, and Balshen Izzet; thank you all so much – any remaining errors are all mine.

None of this would have been possible without the support, encouragement and nagging of Joanna and the KBJ family, especially Lucy King, Heather Winstanley, Megan Hart and the peerless Theia Nankivell, who also recipe-tested my Yorkshire puddings and trialled them on her young twins before giving me the thumbs up.

I've cooked for, and eaten with, so many good friends and colleagues over the years. I can't possibly mention everyone from my time in government and politics – you're all there in the *Speaking Out* acknowledgements – but thankyou to you all, and especially to Gordon Brown who almost certainly features in this book more than he would choose.

Since 2015, I've made new food memories in football grounds across England with the fabulous Delia and Michael and the Norwich City directors; with colleagues in Harvard Square and at El Vino's with the King's teaching team; in restaurants around Piccadilly with Jonny Geller for a pep talk and wise counsel; grabbing lunch with Lord Eric Pickles after a meeting of the Holocaust Memorial Foundation, which we co-Chair; in Strictly arenas and studios with Katya and the gang; in hotels across America and Europe with dedicated and usually exhausted production teams on location; and 5,000 metres up an African mountain for Comic Relief with my fellow climbers. Thank-you to you all.

Some have endured more of my cooking than most.

Acknowledgements

I have been experimenting culinary-wise on our New Year group of friends for 20 years now – Alison and Phil, Brendan and Karen, Bill and Hilary plus all the kids; Steve, Elin and the family in Boston, Mass; and with my oldest friends, Murray and Lois and their boys and Tom and Brigit and their daughters, especially my goddaughter, Rose.

Love and thanks to Yvette's family, David and Alex, Nicky and Andres, all the cousins; and especially the magnificent Tony and June, who have been so generous and supportive to me over the years.

Huge thanks and much love to my sister, Joanna, and brother, Andrew, who both read the first draft, corrected my mistakes and added some stories; and to their partners David and Erica and the cousins.

Much love to my toughest critics: to Yvette, who by retiring from all cooking when our first child was born, gave me no choice really – cook or starve – and whom I love very much; and our three magnificent children who have put up with a lot, and of whom I'm hugely proud.

Above all, love and thanks to my Dad who has suddenly, in his early 80s, become a born-again chef and master of social media food-posting, and has always been there for me. And to my Mum, who was there from the start, passed on everything she had learned about cooking, taught me so much more than just recipes, and who – deep inside – with eyes rolling and her usual mockingly disapproving stare, will, I believe, be proud of how her son turned out. I hope so.

Leftovers

OTHER THINGS I'VE LEARNED ...

My mum and dad were not fans of spicy food when I was
growing up. We had one memorably fiery meal when I was
a child at the home of one of my dad's PhD students, Paul
Moondie. We drove over after eating our usual Sunday roast
lunch for what we thought was afternoon tea to find that
Paul's wife had cooked us an enormous Indian banquet. As
my brother, sister and I exchanged troubled looks, Paul's
wife laughed and said she had sausages and chips waiting
for us and her own kids in the kitchen. My mum and dad
stayed in the dining room and – roast lunch notwithstand-
ing – ploughed their way politely and resolutely through
the entire banquet. My mum didn't stop talking about how
spicy it was for months afterwards.

The idea of cooking Indian, Chinese, Mexican or Thai
food was unheard of back then for a family like ours, despite
the odd restaurant and takeaway popping up in Norwich
and elsewhere. But one day my mum returned from the
supermarket with a packet of chilli con carne spice mix. I

don't know if she meant to pick it up or whether my little brother had slipped it in the trolley, but there it was on the counter – and not to be wasted. My mum didn't make a chilli con carne, of course – that would have been an act of revolution. But she was planning a shepherd's pie that evening and, without telling us, tipped half the spice mix into the mince and onions before topping it with the usual mashed potatoes. Despite the shocked looks on all our faces as we dug in, it tasted amazing; even my dad approved. Chilli con carne shepherd's pie was probably the most exotic thing I'd ever eaten up to that point in my life, and it became a regular in our house.

I learned a vital cooking lesson that day. It was the same old shepherd's pie meat sauce, but, with the extra addition of the spice mix, it was transformed. The same was true with the basic bolognaise sauce my mum had taught me – add pasta sheets and cheese sauce and it became a lasagne. Dial back the tomato purée instead, add cayenne, paprika, cumin, cinnamon and a tin of kidney beans, triple the simmering time, and – Roberto's your uncle – it was a proper chilli con carne. The truth is there's only a relatively small number of basic recipes that a home cook needs to learn – something I'm not sure I fully appreciated until I sat down to write that cookbook for my eighteen-year-old daughter. But if you're willing to innovate, take a risk and make a change, there are so many more varied dishes you can add to your repertoire.

Once you've learned that eggs and yolks, beaten together

with milk or cream and put in the oven, will set firmly enough to be cut with a knife after forty minutes, then you know how to make a cheese pie, a crab and samphire flan or, with some cooked bacon, that '70s favourite, Quiche Lorraine. A simple quesadilla can become a burrito; or an enchilada if you pour over a lasagne-style cheese sauce and bake it for twenty minutes. And a cheese soufflé quickly becomes a haddock soufflé if you simply poach the haddock in the milk you're going to use for your white sauce and then put the fish flakes in the bottom.

Home cooking is all about first learning the basics and then having the confidence to put the recipe books aside and have a go. But there are a few other vital tips that you pick up over the years, a few of which I've included below.

COOKBOOKS

It's so easy these days to find a recipe on the internet – just search lemon meringue pie, chocolate brownies or beef gravy and you're off. And if you put the name of a particular chef in front – Delia's Yorkshire puddings, Mary Berry's salmon en croute, Bobby Flay's quesadilla, Nigel Slater's chicken, Nigella's butter cream – you'll find a recipe that you know will work. But the internet can't replace the vital role cookbooks play, especially when you're looking for inspiration and new ideas or want a visual model for how a dish should ideally look. I love browsing page by page, but with many of my favourite cookbooks there may be only a handful of recipes that I've ever used. Once you've cooked them again and again, added your own variations, modified and perfected the method over decades of trying, and almost certainly forgotten which book you first got the inspiration from, you've had yourself a great bargain.

TASTING

Top chefs say that tasting as you cook is vital. I'm sure they're right, but I've always felt a bit equivocal about this advice. Of course, if you want to get a dish exactly right, then you should test and taste as you go along – a little more salt, a little more pepper – and if you're serving paying customers in a restaurant then you need to know your chefs are getting it right every time. But the downside for the home cook is that tasting as you cook takes away some of the excitement of the big reveal. When I follow a recipe, sometimes I want to wait to taste the final result with everyone else round the table, to see their reactions as I react myself. The more you taste in advance, the less surprise you'll save for yourself.

REPETITION

Again and again and again, repetition is the sure route to success for the home cook. It's hard to get a recipe right the first time, let alone be able to vary things and tailor it to what you or the family want. But repetition makes it so much easier. Do things the same way time after time, then adjust a little bit here, a little bit there, and soon you don't need to refer back to the recipe at all, and you'll probably be surprised by how far you've departed from it when you do. You'll just have found the way that you like to cook, and the way your family enjoys the dish best.

PLANNING AND LISTS

I'm not one for writing out detailed cooking plans. Some people rely on long lists and timing schedules when they're cooking a meal; with my father-in-law, it amounts to a small thesis every time. If you're cooking ten courses, that might be necessary, just because of the risk that something will be forgotten. But personally, I like to hold the plan in my mind and juggle it as I go along, knowing what needs to be done and scrolling back and forth to make sure things are on track. It's brain-training, like doing a sudoku or a crossword. But if you use that kind of method, then you must also use electronic timers. There are only so many balls you can juggle at once, and keeping track of how long something's been cooking is one ball too many.

MISE-EN-PLACE

I don't need a written plan, but I do like to get all my ingredients out, chopped and weighed in advance – it's what proper chefs call a 'mise-en-place'. If you're following a recipe and you're under pressure with time, you don't want to be looking for ingredients and measuring them out as you go along, especially if you've got more than one dish on the go. Much better to have everything prepared and measured in individual bowls or ramekins so that when you're ready to cook it's all there. That way you're much less likely to make mistakes.

INGREDIENTS

Some people swear by the quality of their ingredients, and it's clearly the modern trend in the best restaurants. For the home cook, whether or not you're the grandson of a butcher, quality matters when it comes to meat: finding a good and reliable butcher where you can see what you're buying and know where it's come from is really worth it, and I swear by Farmer Copley's in Pontefract and Meat N16 in Stoke Newington. But at home, I don't think you should get too hung up on this wider ingredients fetish, especially if you're watching your wallet. Yes, different tomatoes can have very different tastes, but most carrots just taste like carrots. And does it really matter what kind of salt you add to a boiling pot? What counts far more for the home cook is knowing your audience – what the family likes, what your guests will enjoy. Innovation is fun, and varying your choice of ingredients can be a part of that. But the taste and food combinations we recognise, know and love are also a hugely important part of family cooking, so if it isn't broke, don't fix it.

PRESENTATION

Should the home cook care about fancy presentation and individual servings? I've always thought family foods should be served in big tureens and doled out, just like they did every evening on *The Waltons*. But if you are cooking recipes which put different elements together at the last minute, like a quesadilla, it's easier to serve on individual plates, restaurant-style. It's also makes sense to serve individually if you are cooking for a family with different needs and tastes: gluten-free, vegetarian mince, no cheese. And it looks better. On this one, I'm in transition.

SURPRISE AND FAMILIARITY

For the restaurant chef, surprise and flair is vital. Amazing ingredients cooked in a novel way and served with panache can take your breath away. One time we went out with a group of old friends – The Millbank Wives (don't ask) – to a Michelin-starred Spanish restaurant in a hotel which looked nothing special from the outside. And although many of the dishes we had that night were special and complex, the one I remember most was a cockle in a small glass with a light clear soup. When you drank it down, it was so fresh and salty, the sensation was like having your head dunked in the sea. When you're preparing food as a form of art, then delivering those kinds of 'experiences' through taste is an achievement in itself.

The home cook, by contrast, is just trying to deliver a great meal, and we know that too much surprise and complexity can get in the way of that. What matters is getting the familiar just right. With a roast dinner, you can get everything else spot-on, but the gravy will make or break the meal. Fish and chips? The batter matters, but if the chips are soggy it's ruined. In a lasagne, you must get the right balance between runnyness and body, and the cheese sauce must be cheesy enough. After fourteen hours of slow cooking, when you break open your pork shoulder, the meat inside either flakes perfectly, or it needs carving and you've fallen short.

That's what makes home cooking so challenging and exciting and sometimes tense. However many times you've made that dish, you never quite know whether today will be the day when it falls short or it's the best you've ever done.

Gadgets

My mum wasn't a big kitchen gadget fan. Despite the Moulinex bought when I was a baby, she tended to mix by hand when she baked. Her knives were old and never very sharp. She did have an astonishing metal contraption, medieval in its horror, into which you put a whole potato and pushed a mesh down and through, slicing the spud into sixteen evenly cut chips. But she'd cook them in a chip pan on the hob, not in a high-tech deep-fat fryer.

She taught me to do most things by hand and – while I've got an electric whisk – nothing beats the satisfaction of successfully whisking under your own steam. One of the highlights of my cooking career was managing to make a cheese soufflé on a boat out at sea. With two forks, and sheer elbow grease, it took me a full hour to get the egg whites to stiff peaks. But it cooked perfectly in the tiny ship's oven; never has a soufflé tasted so good. Recently, however, I have learned to use a fancy food processor with bowl, paddle and multiple speeds, and I must admit I'm wavering. Compared to the challenge of making pastry by hand – trying to keep my hands cold and not over-work the mix – I'm now wondering if I should give in to progress.

OUTDOOR COOKING

I love outdoor-cooking gadgets. My twin-chamber slow-cook BBQ is the best present I've ever received. Twenty years on, it's still going strong, churning out pulled pork shoulders infused with pungent hickory smoke. In recent years, I've also been using a big, egg-shaped, covered BBQ, which uses space-age technology to get your sausages cooked just right. You can fire it up and then shut it down very fast and control the temperature exactly.

My other recent outdoor gadget is a small aluminium pizza oven. Pizza is one of those dishes that is impossible for the home cook to do really well inside in the kitchen because you just can't get the oven hot enough. Either the base feels doughy and undercooked or the top of the ingredients burn while you wait for the yeasty dough to cook. But my outdoor oven burns wood pellets and gets up to twice the heat of a home kitchen oven in just ten minutes. I stretch out my risen dough on a floured paddle, slap on some tomato sauce, mozzarella and a couple of toppings (not more than that or it all goes wrong), slide my pizza into the furnace, and it's cooked in less than a minute. The base will be perfect and crispy, the topping oozing and melting.

Big catering

All those years of constituency BBQs and lunches for seventy at the Morley Labour Rooms have honed my mass-catering skills. These days I love big family celebrations and the logistical challenge of cooking for them. I catered for Yvette's dad's sixtieth birthday and my mum and dad's fiftieth wedding anniversary party and delivered pulled pork sandwiches and treacle tart for over a hundred guests for Yvette's fiftieth birthday in the Queen's Mill in Castleford. The key is to have plenty of time to get everything ready well in advance and do recipes you know like the back of your hand which can easily be cooked at scale.

Every year for nearly two decades now, the same three families have joined us in Castleford for New Year's Eve – eight adults in total plus twelve kids – and it's my job to do the cooking. In the early days that meant fish nuggets or spaghetti bolognaise for the children followed by something fancier for the adults. Now, with the kids all in their teens and twenties, everyone wants to sit and eat the same meal together. It's a struggle to get twenty people around the table, but we manage it every time – including during the pandemic when we had to do it by Zoom. Even as they've become adults, with so many places to go and things to do, they all come back each year for the food and to be together as one big New Year's family.

SHOPPING

I made my solo shopping debut when I was ten years old, after years of apprenticeship accompanying my mum to the local butcher and greengrocer in our village. She taught me to watch the butcher carve the joint, always better than choosing a ready-cut piece, and to watch to see if the meat had the right degree of fat and marbling. I learned to feel the fruit and vegetables, looking out for bruises and limpness.

These days I do most of our shopping on the internet, but with meat I always want to be in the shop to see what they're carving. The best butchers are always happy to let you watch, check and choose, because they know they sell top quality. I also waste many hours I can't afford in department stores, browsing through cookbooks in the books department or walking round the kitchen section. I have two favourites. The basement of any John Lewis store; and the Mecca of many Northern home cooks, the original Lakeland kitchen store in Windermere, where I can easily spend an afternoon comparing Yorkshire pudding tins, pancake pans, whisks and cake moulds.

FRENCH OR ITALIAN

When I was eighteen, and getting ready to head off to university, my mum and dad decided we should go abroad for a holiday, the very first time my sister, my brother and I left the country. We drove down to the south coast and then took the car ferry ride, possibly the most exciting moment of my life thus far, from Portsmouth to Le Havre. We then motored on down to Le Mans, driving on the other side of the road and marvelling at all the little Citroen cars that until then I'd only ever seen in my O Level French vocabulary book, along with real-life signposts for 'La Piscine', 'Le Parc' and 'La Gare'.

We stayed in a tiny village, deep in the Loire Valley, and it didn't rain once. We bought gorgeous French bread from the local village shop and the next-door farmer's wife sold incredibly cheap homemade wine, honey and chickens. We ordered a whole chicken and when I walked over to collect it later that afternoon, I couldn't believe it still had its head and feet on. It turned out my mum was less of a butcher's daughter than we'd all thought and cowered inside along with the rest of us while my dad did the messy business in the garden with a kitchen knife. Needless to say, my little brother had all his vegetarian instincts confirmed.

The supermarkets in France blew our minds. The 'E.Leclerc' hypermarket was huge and had more types of yoghurt than we thought could possibly exist. But the most exciting outings were to local restaurants. My mum had been saving up for months so that we could eat out and have 'Le Menu'. Going out to a restaurant wasn't something that we'd ever done on our English holidays, but, as my mum said, 'When in France ...'

I really enjoyed eating out in France on that trip, but since then our French culinary outings have been a bit hit and miss. The contrast with Italy, where my parents moved just four years after that first French holiday, is striking. Perhaps the Italian cuisine is simpler, and I've had some really great meals in France over the years, especially in top-end restaurants; but the local restaurants I've been to in Italy over the years have been consistently more reliable. And that has also influenced what I cook. I realise now, looking back through this book, that while there are many English, American, Italian and Asian influences, at home I don't often use traditional French recipes. Oh well. *C'est la vie.*

EATING OUT AND ORDERING

Every now and then us home cooks get worn out and need a break. I keep a file of restaurant review cuttings which I add to whenever I see somewhere I'd like to try, or an individual chef or dish getting particular rave reviews. I love restaurant writers, especially the ones who remember to include details of the food among their wider lyrical reflections on life, society and interior decoration.

The world of restaurant-goers divides into risk-takers and safety-firsters when it comes to choosing from the menu, and I'm one of the latter. I like to try new things, but worry that I'll end up regretting missing out on my tried and tested favourites. That is definitely an inheritance from my youth and the rarity of the restaurant experience: the guaranteed luxury of squeezed orange juice versus a step into the bright pink unknown of prawn cocktail!

However, the world of restaurant-goers also divides into those who share and those who don't, and I'm a committed sharer, not least because it allows me to try the new things on someone else's plate while playing safe on my own. When eating out with Yvette, we have a different system. We look at the menu together and discuss what each of us will order, usually something safe we love and something new we fancy the look of. But we have two golden rules: first, that whatever happens, we will swap halfway – no reneging on the deal, no matter how well or badly each other has chosen; and second, when it comes to starters, desserts or side portions, we both must order. There's nothing more frustrating than when your dining partner says, 'I'm full, I'll just try a bit of yours.' So if one of us is going for it, we both do. I won't call it the recipe for a long and happy marriage, but it's worked so far for us.

THAI CHICKEN CURRY

Serves 5

We home cooks need to know when to prepare from scratch and when to leave it to the professionals. Meringues from the shop don't taste as good as the ones you make at home. I've never been to a pub or carvery and had a roast dinner which comes close to the roast dinners that we cook on a Sunday or that my mum cooked before me. But puff pastry? That has to be shop-bought every time. And the same is true with ice cream: however hard I tried, it was never as good as when mass-produced out of a tub. Thai curry paste falls into that same category: you can make the paste at home – I've used the recipe below a few times now and it works – but frankly the experts really know what they're doing. As for the vegetable in the Thai curry, I usually use green beans, but aubergines are also really good.

INGREDIENTS

- 3 chicken breasts, each cut into 8 pieces
- 2 tbsp fish sauce (for marinade)
- 1 tbsp groundnut oil
- 4 tbsp Thai curry paste

Or, if you are going to make your own paste:
- *2 lemongrass stalks, outer layer removed and finely chopped*
- *2 garlic cloves, finely chopped*
- *2cm piece of ginger, peeled and finely chopped (grated if frozen)*
- *½ onion, peeled and finely chopped*
- *3 green chillies, finely chopped*
- *1 tsp ground cumin*
- *2 tbsp fresh coriander, finely chopped*
- *Zest of ½ lime*
- *1 tbsp Thai fish sauce*
- *Good grind of black pepper*

- 400ml can coconut milk
- 200g French green beans or aubergine, chopped
- 1 tbsp fish sauce
- ½ lime
- Handful of coriander, finely chopped

METHOD

1. Pour the marinade fish sauce over the chicken, add a squeeze of lime and leave for half an hour.

2. Heat the oil in a heavy pan, add 4 tablespoons of Thai curry paste. Stir the coconut milk in the tin to emulsify, add 1 tablespoon of the milk to the paste and cook for 3 minutes. Then add the rest of the coconut milk and stir to combine as the mixture heats. (If making your own paste, pulp everything together in a food mixer or by hand in a pestle and mortar.).

3. Add the chicken and the beans/aubergine and bring to a gentle simmer. Add the fish sauce and lime and cook for 7 more minutes. Stir in some fresh, chopped coriander. Transfer to a dish and sprinkle some more coriander on top. Serve with rice.

SWEET & SOUR BEEF BRISKET

Serves 8

I had a short-lived career as a restaurant reviewer. Back in 2017, the *Sunday Times* was looking for people to temporarily fill their prestigious 'Table Talk' restaurant review slot after the passing of A. A. Gill, and asked me to be one of their guest writers. I eagerly agreed and loved the challenge. To be asked to go to some of the most sumptuous restaurants in the country and be paid to write about what I ate – who could complain about that?

I wrote three reviews, sandwiched between the last columns of the acclaimed A. A. Gill and the arrival of the sublime Marina O'Loughlin. The best compliment I had for my reviews was from Delia Smith. 'I enjoyed your reviews,' she told me. 'You actually wrote about the food.'

On my travels for the *Sunday Times*, I visited Skosh in York, a brilliant modern British restaurant with Japanese and Scandinavian influences and The Other Naughty Piglet, a superb French restaurant in London's Victoria. My most memorable trip, however, was to a New York kosher-style deli and diner named Zobler in the old headquarters of the Midland

Bank in the heart of the City of London, now a fancy new hotel. It was an odd experience, eating *kneidlach* and *challah* in an ornate former banking hall. It was made odder by the fact that – despite advertising its Jewish culinary roots – none of the food served was actually kosher, much to the disappointment of my dining companion. But the food was divine – there is nothing quite like New York deli-fare to warm the soul.

I have one recipe I cook regularly that would fit right at home on Zobler's menu – a sumptuous New York sweet and sour beef brisket. It provides enough for eight or more people, and leaves plenty left for lunch for the next few days. It's the kind of dish you can leave in the oven most of the day – this version has a 4½-hour cooking time, but you can easily make it seven hours by cooking at 135°C/250°F/gas mark 1. Always serve it with mashed potato.

INGREDIENTS

- Large piece of beef brisket (approx. 2kg)
- Salt

FOR THE MARINADE

- 2 garlic cloves, peeled and finely chopped
- 1 onion, peeled and finely chopped
- 100ml red wine vinegar
- 75g brown sugar

- 4 tbsp tomato purée
- 2 tbsp paprika
- ½ tsp cayenne pepper
- 1 tbsp soy sauce
- 1 tsp chilli flakes
- 500ml chicken stock

METHOD

1. Preheat the oven to 150°C/300°F/gas mark 2.
2. Put the beef brisket into a large roasting tin and lightly salt all over. Combine all the marinade ingredients and pour all over the beef. Cover with tin foil and bake for 4½ hours.
3. Remove the beef to a serving dish, cover with foil and leave to rest for at least 30 minutes before serving, but longer if you can, and overnight if you wish – time is your friend with brisket. Leave the sauce in the pan to cool and pour off as much of the fat as possible that gathers at the top. If you leave it overnight, it will set.
4. If you have left the brisket to cool slowly for up to an hour, then just reheat the skimmed sauce, pour over the beef and serve; if overnight, then preheat the oven to 170°C/325°F/gas mark 3, put the beef in a dish, pour over the skimmed sauce, cover with foil and leave in the oven for 45 minutes until hot.

Index

Index